Susanna, the Captain and the Castrato

LINDA KELLY has written widely on late eighteenth and
early nineteenth century subjects. Her books include *The Young
Romantics* (also published by Starhaven), *Women of the French
Revolution* and *Richard Brinsley Sheridan*. She is a Fellow of the
Royal Society of Literature and a trustee of the Wordsworth
Trust. Her husband is the writer Laurence Kelly; they live in
London and have three children.

The cover of this book incorporates the only existing likeness
of Susanna Burney as a young woman; the artist of the miniature, probably painted in the year of Susanna's marriage, 1781,
is not known. It is superimposed over a page of her letter-
journals describing the Gordon Riots.

Susanna,

the Captain & the Castrato

Scenes from the Burney Salon
1779-80

Linda Kelly

Starhaven

BUR

ISBN 0-936315-21-0

STARHAVEN, 42 Frognal, London NW3 6AG
in U.S., c/o Box 2573, La Jolla, CA 92038
books@starhaven.org.uk
www.starhaven.org.uk

Typeset in Caslon by John Mallinson
Printed by CPI, 38 Ballard's Lane, London N3 2BJ

Author's note

I owe a special debt of thanks to the British Library for permission to quote from the Burney papers in their possession, in particular Susan (Susanna) Burney's letter journal of 1779-80. Spelling and punctuation follow the original; however, I have used modern spelling and punctuation where dialogue only is concerned and in two cases, as noted in the text, have translated conversations from the French. I am very grateful too, to the Curator of the Berg Collection of English and American Literature, the New York Public Library, Astor and Tilden Foundations, for permission to quote from the Burney papers in the collection; to the ever helpful staff of the London Library and the Kensington and Chelsea Central Library; to my editor Chip Stoddard Martin; to friends and relations who have given me advice and help in various ways: Lesley Blanch, Eliza Chisholm, Rachel Grigg, Shusha Guppy, Jonathan Keates, Rosanna Kelly, the late David Loder, Valerie Pakenham, Mehreen Saigol, Alyson and James Spooner, Oliver Williams and Richard Wilson; and last but certainly not least, to my husband, Laurence Kelly.

Acknowledgements for illustrations can be found on page 139.

To Nathalie

INTRODUCTION

I first came across Susanna Burney when I was writing a book about Juniper Hall, the country house near Mickleham in Surrey, which in 1792-93 provided the unlikely refuge for a group of liberal French aristocrats, including Madame de Staël and Talleyrand, who had fled from France to escape the horrors of the Revolution. Staying in Mickleham with Susanna and her husband Captain Phillips, a veteran of Cook's last voyage, was Susanna's sister, the novelist Fanny Burney. Captivated by their new neighbours, the three soon became friends and confidantes of the French, whose brilliant conversation, illustrious titles and alarmingly progressive morals sent a frisson through local society. The sisters were both shocked and charmed. 'Prim little creatures,' wrote Duff Cooper in his life of Talleyrand, 'they had strayed from the sedate drawing rooms of *Sense and Sensibility* and were in danger of losing themselves in the elegantly disordered alcoves of *Les Liaisons Dangereuses*.'

In writing about this fascinating group it was the letters of the less famous Burney sister, Susanna, many of them still unpublished, that were the real discovery for me. Fluent in French – she had spent two years at school in Paris as a child – she became the special favourite of the Juniper Hall community. For Madame de Staël's lover, the Comte de Narbonne, she was *'la plus douce, la plus spirituelle'* of companions, her sympathy and sensitivity a relief from the possessiveness of his tempestuous mistress. For Fanny Burney, who at the age of forty-one, found true love – but poverty – with Narbonne's great friend General d'Arblay, Susanna was, as she had always been, the

1

most devoted of sisters. It was Susanna who had provided the communicating link between d'Arblay and Dr Burney, whose consternation at the prospect of his elder daughter's marriage to a penniless French exile at first seemed well-founded. But 'never – never,' wrote Fanny, 'was union more exquisitely blessed and felicitous.' Susanna's own marriage was to fall apart soon after, leading indirectly to her early death.

Susanna Phillips was in many ways the pivot of my *Juniper Hall*, a sympathetic go-between in the contrasting love affairs of Madame de Staël and Fanny Burney. The book had not long been published when dining with friends at Covent Garden Opera House one evening, I sat next to Professor Curtis Price, now head of the Royal Academy of Music and author, with Judith Milhous and Robert D. Hume of the classic work, *Italian Opera in Late Eighteenth-Century London*. We talked of Susanna Phillips. 'You know,' he said, 'she was in love with the castrato singer Pacchierotti – it's all in her journal in the British Library.'

I thought no more about it for a time. I was busy with a life of Richard Brinsley Sheridan – incidentally the proprietor of the King's Theatre, Haymarket, London's main opera house during the period, 1779-80, covered by Susanna's diary. I had consulted it briefly, since Susanna was always well up in theatrical gossip and there are amusing comments in it on *The Critic*. But I had not yet gone through its closely written pages – some three hundred and fifty in all – in any detail.

Writing Sheridan's life inevitably plunged me into the world of the eighteenth century theatre, though it was the great actors and actresses of the time – Mrs Siddons, Mrs Jordan, John Philip Kemble – rather than the singers, who held the centre of the stage for him. Still, it was a world I was beginning to know and it was no surprise later on to find how often the name of Sheridan, already a byword for charm and unreliability, recurs in Susanna's diary.

With the book on Sheridan complete, I turned to Susanna Burney and the diary, or rather letter-journals, that eventually became the basis for this book. I spent many hours in the British Library deciphering the faded handwriting and watching Susanna and Pacchierotti's relationship unfold. I was struck by the fluency with which she expressed herself, without crossings-out or second thoughts, and her easy, conversational style; her sister for whom she wrote the letter-journals, is almost a second presence on the page. Gradually I became caught up in her eighteenth century world, the musical evenings at her father's house, the rehearsals and performances at the opera house, her heightened perception of Pacchierotti's presence, whether seen informally at home or glimpsed across a crowded room or theatre. I imagined her writing her journal in snatched moments, away from her stepmother's jealous eyes, in Isaac Newton's old observatory on top of the Burneys' house in St Martin's Street. From here, her knees 'knicky knocky like the Frenchman in *Harlequin's Invasion*', she saw the night sky lit with flames as the Gordon riots surged round them. Her account of those five terrifying days when London was at the mercy of the mob is one of the best first-hand descriptions we have of them.

I was still in the midst of studying Susanna's journal when *The Voyages of Discovery* exhibition at the Natural History Museum in 1999 brought the travels of her future husband, Captain Phillips, vividly to life. One could almost hear the creaking of the rigging and the sound of the wind in the sails as one looked round the section devoted to Captain Cook, marvelling at the beauty and accuracy of the drawings produced in impossibly cramped conditions on board and the awesome range of Cook's achievements. Susanna's brother Jem was with Cook on his second and third voyage round the world. His great friend Lieutenant, later Captain, Phillips, commanded the marines at the time of Cook's murder in Hawaii, distinguishing himself by his bravery on that occasion. Their adventures criss-cross into the story, since Phillips would marry Susanna on his return. With his arrival in London, where he and Jem were greeted as returning heroes, the unspoken romance with Pacchierotti, so delicately recorded in Susanna's journal, comes to a close.

So too does the journal, not to be resumed for several years and never again in such detail. Fuelled by her passionate admiration for the great singer, it survives not only as a fascinating glimpse into the operatic life of late eighteenth century London – 'by far the most important source on opera in the period,' writes Curtis Price – but also as a touching commentary on her relationship with her sister. 'There seems but one soul – but one mind between you,' as Pacchierotti told her, 'you are two in one.' For Fanny Burney she would always be 'the beloved Susanna', a heroine as delightful as any of those in Fanny's own novels though, unlike her counterparts in fiction, Susanna's story, alas, was not to have a happy ending.

I

It used to be said in the eighteenth century that unless a boy joined the navy before the age of puberty he would never be able to stand the hardships of a sailor's life. James Burney, who sailed the world with Captain Cook and ended his career as a rear-admiral, was an example of this theory. The eldest son of the famous musicologist, Dr Charles Burney, he first went to sea as a 'captain's servant' or apprentice at the age of ten. In 1772, aged twenty-two, he joined Cook's second voyage of discovery as a midshipman, later second lieutenant, under Captain Furneaux on board Cook's companion ship, the *Adventure*. In December 1773, after missing a rendezvous at Queen Charlotte's Sound, New Zealand, due to heavy gales, the *Adventure* lost contact with Cook's ship, the *Resolution*, and was forced to return to England alone. She arrived home in July 1774, a year before Cook, bringing with her as a trophy of the voyage the 'noble savage' Omai, a Polynesian from Tahiti, who had asked to join the expedition.

James, or Jem as he was known in the family, had befriended Omai on the voyage, teaching him English as well as learning his own language. Keenly interested in music, like all the Burneys, he also took down the notes of Omai's native instruments and songs. Omai was treated as a celebrity on the *Adventure*'s arrival in England, where his patrons were the celebrated naturalist Joseph Banks and the First Lord of the Admiralty Lord Sandwich. Through them he was introduced into London society: he dined with Dr Johnson at the Thrales's house in Streatham, was painted by Joshua Reynolds and presented to George III, who gave him a pension during his stay in England. In due course he came to dine with Jem and his family at their house in St Martin's Street, arriving directly from the House of Lords where he had been taken to hear the King's speech from the throne. In a letter to a family friend, Samuel Crisp, Jem's sister Fanny gave a vivid picture of the occasion:

'As he had been at Court he was very fine. He had on a suit of Manchester velvet, lined with white satten, a *bag* [wig], lace ruffles and a very handsome sword the King had given him. He is tall and very well made, much darker than I expected to see him, but has a pleasing countenance.

'He makes *remarkable* good bows – not for *him*, but for *anybody*, however long under a Dancing Master's care. Indeed he seems to shame Education, for his manners are so extremely graceful, and he is so polite, attentive and easy, that you would have thought he came from some foreign Court...

'At dinner I had the pleasure of sitting next to him, as my

cold kept me near the fire…He eat heartily and committed not the slightest blunder at table, neither did he do anything *awkwardly* or *ungainly*. He found by the turn of the conversation and some wry faces, that a joint of beef was not roasted enough, and therefore when he was helped, he took great pains to assure mama that he liked it, and said two or three times *"very dood* – very *dood."*

'I assure you everybody was delighted with him…' concluded Fanny. 'The conversation of our house has turned ever since upon Mr *Stanhope* [Lord Chesterfield's son] and *Omai* – the first with all the advantages of Lord Chesterfield's instructions, brought up at a great school, introduced at fifteen to a Court, taught all possible accomplishments from an infant…and proved after it all a meer *pedantic booby* – the second with no tutor but Nature, changes, after he is grown up, his dress, his way of life, his diet, his country and his friends; and appears in a *new world* like a man [who] had all his life studied *the Graces.*'

The household to which Jem returned was a crowded one, lively with streams of visitors as well as members of the family. In the autumn of 1774 the Burneys, who had been living in Queen's Square, had moved to a new house in St Martin's Street, an area of small shops and industries off Leicester Fields, now Leicester Square. Formerly owned by Sir Isaac Newton, it boasted Newton's old observatory, a glass-sided turret at the top of the house with widespreading views over London, and a spacious first floor drawing room whose folding doors opened onto the library, a room which doubled as a music room and contained two harpsichords. All the family, as has been said, were passionately fond of music. At the time of Jem's return from sea the household consisted of Dr Burney, his second wife, formerly Mrs Stephen Allen, Dr Burney's three daughters by his first marriage, Fanny, Susanna and Charlotte, and

Dr and Mrs Burney's two children, Dick and Sarah Harriet. Dr Burney's eldest daughter Esther (Hetty) had married her first cousin, the musician Charles Rousseau Burney and lived nearby in Tavistock Street; his second son Charles was away at Charterhouse. Of Mrs Burney's children by her former marriage, two were already married; another was studying in France.

There must have been relief as well as pride among the Burneys that Jem had survived the hazards of his two year voyage: violent gales off the Cape of Good Hope in which almost all the livestock had been swept overboard; the risks of scurvy and sickness; long periods of shortage of water; the fogs and snows of the Antarctic, where the ships were in constant danger of being crushed by icebergs; the fruitless search for the *Resolution* in the second of two separations from their sister ship. He had also been personally involved in a horrifying episode, in some ways prophetic of Cook's murder four years later. It took place off Queen Charlotte's Sound, where the *Adventure*, after failing to meet up with Cook, had spent two weeks refitting, apparently on good terms with the local inhabitants. On the eve of their departure the captain, Tobias Furneaux, sent a cutter with ten men ashore to collect some supplies of green stuff for the voyage.

'They were ordered to return at three o'clock,' wrote Fanny, recounting the story to Crisp; 'but upon their failure Captain Furneaux sent a launch, with Jem to command it, in search of them. They landed at two places without seeing anything of them…Jem says he imagined they were gone further up the country, but never supposed how *very* long a way they were gone. At the third place, it is almoſt too terrible to mention, they found –'

Fanny's pen stops here, leaving the rest of her page blank, as if she could not face giving further details. We must leave it to Captain Furneaux, in his laconic report of the episode, to complete the tale:

'He [Burney] returned at 11 o'Clock the same night with the melancholy news of…being cut off by the Indians in Grass Cove where they found the Relicks of several and the intrails of five men lying on the beach and in the Canoes they found several baskets of human flesh and five odd shoes new, as our people had been served Shoes a day or two before; they brought on board several hands, two of which we knew, one belonged to Thomas Hill being marked on the back T.H. another to Mr Rowe who had a wound on his fore finger not quite whole, and the head, which was supposed was the head of my servant by the high forhead he being a Negroe…'

Despite this gruesome experience, Jem was all eagerness to join a further voyage to the Antipodes should the opportunity arise. Meanwhile, in January 1775 he was appointed as second lieutenant on the *Cerberus*, a twenty-eight gun frigate bound for North America, where the clouds of rebellion were building up and naval reinforcements were required. The ship, it seems, was not a happy one; the crew was unsatisfactory, and there was a general feeling of sympathy with the rebellious colonists. 'Their ſtay is quite uncertain,' wrote Fanny when the *Cerberus* left Portsmouth. 'Jem prays for his return in time to go to the South Seas. He says that if they have fine weather they shall have a jovial voyage – but if bad – God help them and all these useless hands!'

With the departure of Jem to America, taking with him a whiff of sea air and adventure, the household in St Martin's Street settled down to its normal routine. Everyday life was far from being boring where the Burneys were concerned, for the recent publication of Dr Burney's journals of his travels in Germany and Italy had made him a celebrity, and he was now embarked on a more ambitious project, an encyclopædic general history of music; the first volume, dedicated to Queen Charlotte, would be published the following year. A small extension beyond the music room, where he still took pupils to support his family, had become his work-place. The desk and shelves of this study were piled with his 'chaos of materials'; his daughter Fanny acted as his amanuensis, copying and recopying his disordered manuscripts for many hours each day. His next daughter, Susanna, was an accomplished musician, both as a singer and on the harpsichord; presumably, her musical studies were considered important, and it was Fanny, less obviously talented, who bore the brunt of her father's secretarial work.

Fanny was a devoted secretary and copyist, but unbeknownst to her elders she was already embarked on a project of her own, her novel *Evelina*, written in whatever moments of leisure she could snatch, with her sisters Susanna and Charlotte as her chief confidantes and editors. The story has something of a Cinderella quality. A beautiful young orphan – perhaps Fanny was thinking of her own motherless state – makes her entry into the world at the age of seventeen. Innocent and inexperienced, she is thrown up against the vices and follies of London society, maintaining her virtue and integrity through a series of embarrassments and vicissitudes. A crowd of characters spring to life around her: her vulgar French grandmother, all wrinkles and rouge; her boorish social climbing cousins; her long-lost father, who refuses to acknowledge her; a coarse sea captain; a titled fop, whose insolence makes her life a misery; a ragged and despairing Scottish poet; and last but not least the romantic Lord Orville, whom she marries after many ups and downs.

Once started, the story unfolded at a rattling pace, its freshness and gaiety sounding a new note in eighteenth century literature. By the time that Jem returned from America, with the rank of First Lieutenant, in January 1776, Fanny had completed the first two volumes and using her younger brother Charles as an intermediary, was beginning to negotiate with a publisher. Jem may well have been let into the secret, but his own affairs were moving too fast to spend much time on his sister's. Thanks to the influence of Lord Sandwich, he had been offered the chance of a place on Cook's next voyage. As before, two ships were involved, the *Resolution*, under Captain Cook, and the *Discovery*, under Captain Charles Clerke, a brilliant and experienced officer who had served on Cook's two previous voyages of exploration.

The expedition was to due to leave in early summer, and among its aims was the return of Omai to 'such one of the South Sea Islands as he may desire'. Its principal objective however, was to seek a northern passage by sea from the Pacific to the Atlantic Ocean. Cook's official instructions were to travel southward from the Cape of Good Hope, and thence via New Zealand to Tahiti and the Society Islands. From there he was to proceed to the North American coast, travelling northwards as far as the latitude of 65 degrees, or further, 'if not obstructed by land or ice'. In the event of not finding a passage, he was to spend the winter in Kamchatka, before proceeding further northward the following spring to continue the search for a sea route from east to west.

Jem was to serve on the smaller of the two ships, the *Discovery*, under Captain Clerke. Among his fellow officers were the sailing master William Bligh, the future commander of the *Bounty*; Cook's third lieutenant, John Williamson, a difficult and unsatisfactory character, who would cause nothing but trouble on the voyage; and a tall, good looking, rather idle young Irishman, Lieutenant, later Captain, Molesworth Phillips, who commanded the expedition's contingent of thirty marines.

Omai made a farewell visit to the Burneys before leaving London, impressing Fanny once again with his good manners, and remarking with a bow that Jem was a 'very *dood man*'. He seemed genuinely sad at the thought of parting with his friends, Cook noted later, but his eyes sparkled with joy whenever the conversation turned to his native land. He was returning home laden with presents, great riches in his countrymen's eyes, and once on board ship he seemed perfectly happy.

On June 15, 1776 the *Discovery* set sail from Deptford to Plymouth, in preparation for the voyage. Jem was temporarily in command, for Clerke had been detained in London in a debtor's prison for an unpaid debt of his brother's and was only able to join them when Cook had already sailed. The two ships were to rendezvous at the Cape. Fanny was proud of Jem's involuntary promotion. 'The great Man of Men is your friend James, who is now, in *fact* and in *power*, Captain of his ship, though, alas! not in *honour* or *profit*,' she wrote to Crisp. It was the last time, for a long time, that she or her family would have any direct news of her brother.

II

By October 1776 the *Resolution* and the *Discovery* had met up at Table Bay. They set sail together on December 1, in constant anxiety of being separated by fogs or heavy seas, spending Christmas at Christmas Harbour, on the desolate sub-Antarctic island of Kerguelen, with roast penguin as the main dish of the day. On December 30, they set out for Tasmania (then known as Van Diemen's Land) and New Zealand, then lingered for several months in the Friendly Islands before sailing to Tahiti. Here Omai was welcomed with due honour and, after some negotiations with the local chieftains, was installed on the neighbouring island of Hulaheine, where the ships' carpenters built him a house, with a well stocked garden and a paddock for his animals: ducks, geese, pigs, two horses, and a goat in kid.

Before leaving on November 3 Cook gave private instructions to Omai that if all was going well with him, he should send him two white beads at his next destination on the island of Ulaietea; if indifferently two brown beads; if he was ill used or in distress the signal was to be two blue beads. There were moving farewells at the moment of parting, Omai, according to Jem, shedding tears of 'real and unaffected sorrow' at leaving his old friends. Nine days later he was able to record with satisfaction in his journal that 'some canoes from Hulaheine brought us an account of Omai being in good health and living in harmony with his neighbours'. The happy news had been confirmed by the arrival of Omai's own sailing canoe, with four white beads. It was the end of a curiously poignant episode in which Jem, who had befriended Omai from the first, had played a consistently sympathetic role.

With Omai safely delivered home, Cook pressed northward, spending Christmas at a waterless coral atoll, fitly christened Christmas Island. They left there on January 2, 1778, hoping to find water when they reached the northwest coast of North America, or New Albion as it was known. Two weeks later the look-out, James Ward, gave a cry of 'Land!' He was the first European to set eyes on the Hawaiian, or Sandwich Islands, as Cook christened them; a whole new area of the Pacific had been opened up to Western navigators. As they approached the great volcanic island of Kauai, a fleet of canoes came out to meet them. When their suspicions had been dispelled by gifts and friendly gestures, Jem called down in Polynesian to the men in the leading canoe asking the name of their island. It was a happy surprise to find that they not only spoke the same language but, as they later discovered, shared many of the customs of the Tahitians. A shore party under Williamson was sent to reconnoitre for an anchorage. Almost before his boat touched the beach, he was surrounded by a crowd of excited Hawaiians and, losing his head, fired off a shot, killing one of their leaders. It was a 'cowardly, dastardly action', according to the ship's corporal, and an omen of how little his judgement could be trusted. Despite this bad beginning however, the natives proved friendly and hospitable, and a brisk trade, with nails and axes in exchange for food, was soon established. It would have been pleasant to linger in the mild sub-tropical climate of the islands, but Cook was impatient to reach the Arctic during the summer months, and they stayed only long enough to take on water and supplies. He intended to explore them more fully on return.

On January 29, 1778, while Jem and his companions were savouring the thrill of discovery on the far side of the world, an advertisement appeared in several of the London newspapers:

This day was published
EVELINA
or a Young Lady's Entrance into the World
Printed for T. Lowndes, Fleet-Street

In her memoirs of her father Fanny describes how her step-mother, who was glancing through the newspaper at breakfast, unsuspectingly read out the announcement before passing on to other articles: 'Had she lifted her eyes from the page, some-thing more than suspicion must have met them, from the con-scious colouring of the scribbler, and the irresistible smiles of the two sisters, Susanna and Charlotte, who were present.'

Mrs Burney had been a rich widow when Dr Burney married her, and her money had done much to help the fam-ily. But she was a jealous and demanding character, heartily detested by her step-children, who christened her 'La Dama' and took care to conceal all matters of importance from her. Their secret, however, could not be kept for long. The growing success of *Evelina* made it impossible for Fanny to retain her anonymity. Gradually, partly through word of mouth, partly through favourable notices in the press, the book became a best-seller (though having paid the author a lump sum of £20, it was Lowndes, the publisher, who kept the profit). Burke stayed up all night to finish it, Dr Johnson growled approval, and one of Lowndes's lady customers complained that she was regarded as unfashionable because she had not read it. The story of its authorship, at first revealed only to her family and a few close friends, crept out and Fanny at the age of twenty-five, found herself on a pinnacle of fame. Petted and feted by the great, from Burke to Sheridan and Reynolds, she was taken up especially by the celebrated Mrs Thrale, wife of the wealthy brewer Henry Thrale, and the patron and beloved friend of Dr

Johnson.

Dr Burney was already an intimate of the Thrale household at Streatham Park, where he went each week to give music lessons to their eldest daughter Queeney, usually staying on for the night to take part in whatever social life was going. Mrs Thrale took an instant fancy to Fanny, though not without a touch of aristocratic condescension. 'She is a graceful girl, but 'tis the grace of an actress, not a woman of fashion – how could it [be]', she wrote in her diary *Thraliana*. But on the whole she was pleased to welcome a new celebrity to Streatham Park, where Dr Johnson, feeling himself privileged by his age, made much of the modest young authoress, calling her his pet, his little Burney, his little character-monger, and enveloping her in bear-like hugs.

The house in St Martin's Street was crowded; Fanny shared a cramped room with her sisters and had no place of refuge but the draughty observatory on top of the house. Even though her stepmother had grudgingly praised her book, she remained an unfriendly and oppressive presence. To escape to the comforts and good company of Streatham Place, and to bask for a while in the glow of her success, was a welcome prospect. Mrs Thrale was pressing; Dr Burney, sensing advantage for his daughter, was pleased to part with her; and for much of 1779 and 1780, Fanny became a member of the Thrale household, sometimes installed at Streatham, sometimes travelling with them to the holiday towns of Bath and Brighton. Susanna, her favourite sister, the 'companion of my heart' in Fanny's words, was left behind in London. It is thanks to this separation that we have the series of enchanting letter-journals she exchanged with Fanny during this period.

In the absence of her brothers and her elder sisters (Esther much occupied with her own young family) Susanna had become an important figure in her father's musical salon.

A fine musician herself, she also spoke fluent French and some Italian and so was well placed to deal with the stream of foreign celebrities, composers and singers who gathered in her father's drawing room. Her stepmother, La Dama, though a lively conversationalist, was only an indifferent linguist. Dr Burney, on the other hand, having travelled throughout Europe in pursuit of musical knowledge, was at ease in several languages, above all in Italian, the language of opera at the time.

Dr Burney's social position was peculiar. He made his living as a music teacher and, in the words of Macaulay, 'belonged in fortune and in station to the middle class'. Yet few nobles in the grandest mansions of St James's Street or Grosvenor Square could assemble around them so brilliant and varied a company as was sometimes to be found in Dr Burney's modest dwelling in St Martin's Street. He himself was the most delightful of companions. 'I love Burney. My heart goes out to him,' said Dr Johnson, and Johnson was only one of the lions that gathered in his drawing room.

Accustomed since childhood to her father's lively circle, with its mix of grandees, writers and performing artists, Susanna Burney's social experience was far wider than that of most well brought-up young women of the day. She was twenty-four when she wrote her letter-journals, two years younger and to judge from her portrait miniature, much prettier than her sister: bright eyed, with delicate features and a mouth just curving into a smile. Much loved by her family, she had a sweetness of disposition that showed itself from an early age. There is a characteristic story of her visiting the theatre when she was very young. The play was *Jane Shore*, and when the supposedly starving heroine paced the stage, declaring that she had not eaten for three days, it was too much for the little girl. 'Then ma'am,' she declared, 'please to accept of my orange', handing it to her from the stage box.

There was never any question of jealousy of her elder sister, and she took a whole-hearted delight in her success. But there was nothing cloying or insipid about her. Not only was she highly intelligent, sharing Fanny's gifts of observation, ear for dialogue and delight in the absurd, but her knowledge and love of music, as the great castrato singer Pacchierotti remarked, made her capable of judging it *en professeur*. Thanks to her father's connections, she had almost unlimited access to the King's Theatre, Haymarket, the main venue for Italian opera and her journals for the season of 1779-80, with their detailed reportage of performances and conversations with performers – Pacchierotti in particular – open a unique window on the operatic life of the time.

The first entries, however, take place before the opening of the opera season. They recount a visit to the Thrales at Streatham Place, and afterwards to Chesington Hall, the home of Samuel Crisp, where Susanna and her father were to stay for a few days. Fanny was in London, looking after their sister Esther who had recently suffered a miscarriage, but was now recovering. Relieved of his immediate worries, Dr Burney set out for Streatham in a high good humour which Susanna, though less happy about her sister's health, did her best not to dispel. It was pleasant August weather, and Susanna's first sight of Streatham Place, a large white house with a paddock round it, surpassed all her expectations.

'The Avenue to the House – Plantations &c. are beautiful – worthy of the charming inhabitants – it is a little Paradise I think – Cattle – Poultry – Dogs all running freely about without *annoying* each other!'

They found Mrs Thrale with Dr Johnson sitting late over breakfast in the library. Mrs Thrale rose to greet them, a small pretty woman in her late thirties, with great liveliness of manner. After welcoming Susanna 'most sweetly' to Streatham, she went to find a poem for Dr Burney, which Dr Johnson wished to show him. As soon as she was gone Dr Johnson invited her to sit next to him.

"'Come – come here my Little Dear" sd. he with great kindness – & took my hand as I sat down. I then took courage to deliver your Respects "Aye – why don't she come among us?" sd. he – I sd. you were confined by a sick sister but that you were very sorry to be away. "A Rogue" sd. he laughing – "she don't mind Me!"'

When it was time for Dr Burney to give Queeney her music lesson, Mrs Thrale took Susanna round the house and grounds.

'She took me in your Room – shewed me your Desk – then her own Dressing Room & Miss Streatfield, Miss Thrale & Miss Burney over the Chimney piece – "they are three pretty Misses, that they are" sd. she – I then went into her Bed Room – & into the other wch. is much yours – "You see we *live* together" sd. she "& Streatham is not Streatham without her. We *do* miss her sadly that's the truth on't."' Throughout the visit, Susanna noted, Mrs Thrale looked at her with great curiosity; she had grown possessive about Fanny and, though she behaved with the 'utmost politeness', may well have been jealous of her closeness to her younger sister.

After wandering about the gardens and plantations, talking of Fanny and of Esther's health – 'she was extremely pleased Dr Broomfield had been applied to' – they returned to the house and went into the music room. Queeney Thrale, 'coldly civil as usual', sang a song, *In te spero*. 'I was better pleased than I expected to be with hearing her,' wrote Susanna; 'her voice is very sweet & wll. improve with practice…however – "Manca l'anima – e l'anima sempre Mancara!"' Dr Burney then played through some songs from a new opera, the *Olimpiade*. While he was playing Dr Johnson came with a book in his hand to show Dr Burney, but seeing him busy went up to Susanna who was standing near the piano:

'He put his arm round me, & smiling at me very good humouredly sd. "Now you don't expect me that I shall ever love you so well as I do your Sister?" – "Oh No Sir" – sd. I – "I have no such hopes – I am not so presumptious" – "I'm glad you're so *Modest*" sd. he laughing – & so encouraged was I by his good humour (& he kept *see sawing* me back and forwards in his arms as if he had taken me for you) that I told him I must make an interest with him *through you* – he again sd. he was glad I was so *Modest* – & added – "but I believe you're a good little Creature – I think I should love *you* too if *one did but know you!*" There's for you – I assure you I shall set this little conversation down among my first honours – it put me in good humour & spirits for the rest of the day.'

They left Streatham Place, laden with gifts of fruit for their host at Chesington Hall. 'Don't expect me to love you so well as your sister,' Dr Johnson repeated comically to Susanna as she left, but added a 'very good natured farewell' – *"Goodbye my little love"*.

Samuel Crisp was one of the Burneys' oldest friends, devoted to all the family, in particular to Fanny, who called him 'Daddy Crisp' and regaled him with some of her most amusing letters. Once a fashionable man about town, Crisp was now an elderly recluse, soured by failures in the world of letters, and his house in the depths of Surrey, approached by a cart track over a desolate common, was as lonely and remote as it was possible to imagine. But the Burney children loved the house, with its nooks and crannies and dark passages 'leading to nothing', its tapestries and blue-tiled fireplaces, and its elderly hostesses Kitty Cook and Mrs Hamilton who kept house for him. Since Crisp was short of money, he allowed a few favoured friends such as the Burneys to stay there on an expense-sharing basis.

The great entertainment of the Burneys' stay at Chesington was a reading from the manuscript of Fanny's play, *The Witlings*, written at the request of Richard Brinsley Sheridan, then manager of Drury Lane. Dr Burney was the reader, amid judicious praise from Crisp – 'It's funny, it's funny indeed' – and virtual incomprehension from Mrs Hamilton and Kitty Cook, who had been under solemn promises to be silent during the reading. 'And indeed, poor souls, both might as well have been away for all they understood of the matter…' wrote Susanna, 'but when it was all over Kitty turned to Mrs Gast [Crisp's sister] & Me & sd. – "She's *very clever!* – isn't she" – I was too modest to answer but by laughing.'

Fanny's play, a skit on the pretensions of the Blue Stockings, was never performed. Her father, though he praised it warmly, felt it would cause too much offence to that powerful coterie of learned ladies to be acceptable. Samuel Crisp agreed, and Fanny, deeply disappointed, was prevailed on to abandon it. Meanwhile Susanna's pleasant stay at Chesington was disturbed by alarming public news. In June 1779 Spain had followed France's lead in recognising American independence and declaring war on Britain. Suddenly in August the French and Spanish fleets had been sighted in the Channel. Their plan was to sweep westward, clearing the waters of all British ships; behind them, the French army could then be rushed across the Channel. All through August the British fleet was in retreat, and rumours of invasion proliferated.

'Two days [ago],' wrote Susanna on August 29, 'a report reached us from Kingston…that the French and Spaniards were landed at Falmouth, while the combined Fleets were throwing bombs into Plymouth – Mr Crisp who spends all his life in perpetual apprehension of terrible natural Calamities, went into Kingston the next morng. – & came back with a Countenance calculated to terrify and crush Temerity itself

– He cd. eat no Dinner – and seemed ſtruck with such a con-
ſternation that the moſt impenetrable Creature muſt have felt
something at seeing him…He supposed that troops of French
wd. march to London and pass through Kingſton – Death and
Desolation would attend their ſtep – in short everything that
cd. be apprehended He was prepared to expeƈt…This day and
the next we spent really miserably – Poor Mr Crisp cd. neither
eat, sleep or talk – Sunday we recd. intelligence from our father
[who had left two days earlier]…which produced a *Revolution*
in our *minds* – for we then found that the French had not yet
attempted to land, or attack any part of the kingdom, & that
tho' much was to be dreaded there yet remained something to
Hope – after Tea we took a comfortable walk wch. made us
some amends for our late dismalities.'

On the walk they passed a gipsy encampment, where a
pretty young gipsy with a pipe in her mouth offered to tell
their fortunes. Mr Crisp was so captivated by her dark skin,
white teeth and sparkling eyes that alarums and invasions
were forgotten and he could hardly tear himself away. By the
following evening he had so far recovered his spirits that he
allowed himself to be dressed up in Susanna's cap, with his wig
turned round beneath it, and dance a minuet, pretending to be
Madame Duval, the vulgar French grandmother in *Evelina*.

III

Between August and mid-October 1779 there were no more letters from Susanna to Fanny, or at least none that have been preserved. By late September the invasion scare had died away, when a virulent outbreak of smallpox among the enemy fleets forced them to put back into the French ports. The public breathed again, and Richard Brinsley Sheridan put the finishing touches to his satire on heroic tragedy, *The Critic*, with its play within a play, based on the impending invasion of England by the Spanish Armada. Fanny went on an extended visit to Brighton with the Thrales, while in London Dr Burney toiled away at the second volume of his history of music – Susanna, we may imagine, doing some of Fanny's work as his secretary and copyist. No one had heard any news of Jem, but he must often have been in their thoughts and conversation. The extraordinary interest aroused by Captain Cook's great voyage extended to all those sailing with him and cast its reflected glamour on those concerned with them. Both sisters were intensely proud of their adventurous sailor brother, little knowing the tragedies that had befallen him and his companions.

On leaving the Sandwich Islands in February 1778, the *Resolution* and the *Discovery* had made their way to the west coast of America (or New Albion), about which very little was known from the latitude of 40 degrees. Travelling northward, they made an almost continuous survey of the coast line, then rounding Alaska, pressed on through the Bering Strait, and entered the Arctic Sea. On August 15, at just over 69 degrees north, their way was blocked by a solid wall of ice, stretching from horizon to horizon, and they knew that they could go no further. Though they had failed to find a northern passage, it had been an amazing voyage of discovery, during which more than a thousand miles of intricate and unknown coastline had been surveyed and charted. It is pleasing to record that among their discoveries was an island in the Bering Strait, which Cook named Burney Island.

The expedition was to winter in the Sandwich Islands. They arrived there in late November, discovering two new islands, the second of which, Hawaii, with its spectacular coastline and snow topped mountains, was by far the largest they had found in the Pacific. On January 17, 1779, they anchored in Karakakooa Bay, on the west coast of Hawaii. Dominating the bay was a great cliff, at the foot of which was a Tahitian style *morai*, or sacred place, with carved images and skulls on poles, surrounded by a dilapidated fence. The bay had a special significance in Polynesian mythology: tradition had it that one day the god Orono, presiding deity of the festival of the harvest, would appear there in a 'great canoe'. By an extraordinary coincidence, Cook had arrived at the place foretold at exactly the moment of the festival, as though in fulfilment of the legend. Throughout his stay he was greeted as Orono, regarded with something close to adoration and, despite 'persistent thieving' from the natives, was given every help in refitting and trading for supplies.

On February 4, the ships left Hawaii laden with provisions and with lavish gifts of feathered cloaks for Cook. They had only been gone four days when they ran into a gale in the course of which one of the *Resolution's* masts was so badly damaged that they were forced to put back into Karakakooa Bay for repairs. This time they found a very different reception. The Hawaiians had already parted with more food than they could spare. Their chiefs were suspicious, stones were thrown at the sailors while they were working and the problems of thieving increased dramatically. On the morning of February 14 it was found that the *Discovery's* large cutter had been stolen during the night. Cook determined on firm measures. After sending boats to blockade the bay, he set off with Phillips and a party of eight marines, intending to take the ruler of the islands, King Terre'aboo, as a friendly hostage until the cutter was returned.

The events of the next few hours have often been told, but since both Jem and Molesworth Phillips are heroes of our story, we will follow what happened, where possible, through their eyes. While Phillips accompanied Cook to the shore, Jem remained on board the *Discovery*. Through his spy-glass he could see Cook and his party disappearing up the path to the village where Terre'aboo lived; the launch that had brought them stood by with a pinnace and a cutter just off shore. They had scarcely set off when there was a sound of musket fire from the bay. The boats blockading it had become involved in a skirmish with several large canoes which were trying to escape, and in the course of the firing an important chief was killed.

The news reached the village just as Cook and his marines brought Terre'aboo to the beach, where a huge crowd had begun to gather. The King had agreed quite amiably to accompany Cook on board. However just as he was preparing to embark one of his wives and two chiefs caught hold of him, tearfully begging him not to go; at the same time the crowd began to murmur ominously. 'It was at this period we first began to suspect that they were not very well disposed to us,' wrote Phillips, 'and the marines being huddled together in the midst of an immense mob composed of at least two or three thousand people, I proposed to Captain Cook that they might be arranged in order along the rocks by the water side, which he approving of, the crowd readily made way for them and they were drawn up accordingly. We now clearly saw they were collecting their spears, etc., but an awful rascal of a priest was singing and making a ceremonious offering to the Captain and Terre'aboo to divert their attention from the manouevres of the surrounding multitude.'

Cook now gave up all thoughts of taking Terre'aboo, observing to Phillips that he could 'never think of compelling him to go aboard without killing a number of these people'. He was just about to give the order to embark, when he was threatened by a man armed with a long iron spike, or pah'hoo'ah, and fired at him with small shot, doing the man no harm but provoking the crowd still further. Another man, also carrying a spike, was driven off by Phillips with the butt of his gun. Stones were thrown, knocking down one of the marines, and Cook then fired a ball and killed a man.

'They now made a general attack,' continued Phillips, 'and the Captain gave orders to the marines to fire and afterwards called out, "Take to the boats". I fired just after the Captain and loaded again whilst the marines fired. Almost instantaneously upon my repeating the orders to take to the boats, I was knocked down by a stone, and in rising received a stab with a pah'hoo'ah in the shoulder; my antagonist was on the point of seconding his blow when I shot him dead. The business was now a most miserable scene of confusion. The shouts and yells of the Indians far exceeded all the noise I ever came in the way of. These fellows, instead of retiring upon being fired upon, as Captain Cook and I believe most people concluded they would, acted so very contrary a part, that they never gave the soldiers time to re-load their pieces, but immediately broke in upon and would have killed every man of them, had not the boats by a smart fire kept them a little off, and picked up those who were not too wounded to reach them. After being knocked down I saw no more of Captain Cook. All my people I observed were totally vanquished, and endeavouring to save their lives by getting to the boats. I therefore scrambled as well as I could into the water, and made for the pinnace which I fortunately got hold of, but not before I received another blow from a stone just above the temple, which had not the pinnace been very near, would have sent me to the bottom.'

Phillips's report, drawn up immediately after his return on board the *Resolution*, ends here. He had not witnessed Cook's death, which Jem and Captain Clerke, unable to help since all the boats were gone, were desperately watching through their glasses. The last time Cook was seen distinctly he was standing on the water's edge, gesturing to the boats to pull in. No one had offered him any violence while he faced the crowd, but on turning to give orders to the boats he was stabbed in the back and fell face down into the water. On seeing him fall the islanders set up a great shout, and his body was immediately dragged on the shore, where it was cut to pieces by the crowd.

Four of Phillips' marines had been killed, three more were dangerously wounded. One of them, a poor swimmer, was saved by Phillips, who seeing him struggling in the water, threw himself overboard despite his wounds and dragged him to the pinnace by his hair. Barely conscious, but realising that the pinnace would be dangerously overloaded if he stayed on board, Phillips then jumped back into the water and made for the small cutter which was standing by.

In contrast to Phillips's gallantry, Williamson, commanding the launch on which Cook and the marines had landed, proved to be the villain of the piece. Choosing to interpret Cook's signals as a order to retreat, he had ordered his crew to row away from the shore, instead of coming to the rescue. His men were outraged by this decision, but he forbade them to come into firing range, even threatening to shoot the first man who fired a shot. It is entirely possible that had Williamson backed up the other two boats with extra fire power, Cook's murder might have been avoided. In the aftermath of Cook's death, Williamson was regarded with almost universal contempt and by Phillips with a hatred that led to challenging him to a duel. Another officer, probably Jem, put a stop to it before any harm was done.

Meanwhile the lives of all the expedition hung in the balance, though it soon became clear that the Hawaiians were as appalled by what had happened as the English were. One of the most moving moments in the uncertain days that followed was when two young Hawaiians, armed with spears, swam out to the *Discovery* to sing a lament for Orono beneath the stern. After about fifteen minutes of this song, listened to with professional interest by Jem, who was officer of the watch, the Hawaiians climbed aboard and presented him with their spears in atonement for Orono's death, then dived off the side and swam back to shore.

Jem, in a grisly mission recalling his earlier experiences off Queen Charlotte's Sound, was sent ashore with Cook's second lieutenant, James King, to negotiate for the recovery of the bodies of Captain Cook and the marines. All of the corpses had been burned, and those of the marines were irretrievable, but the bones of Captain Cook were ceremonially delivered to the *Resolution* a few days later. Having been put into a coffin, and a service read over them, they were committed to the deep with all military honours. 'What our feelings were on this occasion,' wrote King, 'I leave to the world to conceive; those who were present know it is not in my power to express them.'

IV

The death of Captain Cook left Jem's commander Captain Clerke in charge of the expedition. But further tragedy lay ahead for Clerke, who had picked up the seeds of consumption in the debtors' prison, was already desperately ill. As the expedition travelled northwards from the Sandwich Islands in a second attempt to find a northern passage to Europe, Clerke knew that his death was only a matter of time. He consigned the task of navigation to the twenty-eight year old William Bligh, the finest navigator on either ship. 'However tarnished his reputation may have become in later years,' writes Cook's biographer Richard Hough, 'nothing can diminish the sublime nature of his [Bligh's] navigating skills from the Arctic to Petropavlosk, to Macao, thence to the Cape and home via Stromness in the Orkney islands.'

Clerke died on August 22, 1779. With the ships in bad repair, and their way once more blocked by ice in the Arctic Sea, he had already decided that the expedition should make for home. Jem now became first lieutenant on the *Resolution*, under Cook's former first lieutenant Captain Gore; King was given command of the *Discovery*, with Williamson as his first lieutenant. After refitting in Kamchatka, they reached Macao on December 1 and heard for the first time that Britain was at war with France and the North American states. (They had not yet heard the news of war with Spain.) With the possibility of capture in mind Jem made a copy of his journal on china paper, small enough to be concealed so that, in the event of the official journals being lost, a record could be preserved for the

Admiralty. Written in a microscopic hand, so tiny that it could only be read with a magnifying glass, it is now in the British Library.

The news of Cook's death, sent overland from Kamchatka, would not reach London till January 1780. Meanwhile the great event of the autumn for the Burney household was the arrival of the celebrated castrato singer Gasparo Pacchierotti, who had been engaged for the season at the King's Theatre, Haymarket.

For most of the eighteenth century the castrato, or *musico* as he was known, was the *prima donna* of the age; traditionally cast as the operatic hero, he was far more important than the leading tenor or soprano and correspondingly better rewarded. Already a star in Italy, Pacchierotti had made his English début the previous year and had been greeted with immense enthusiasm. Idolised by London society, swooned over by female admirers, he had found a calmer refuge in Dr Burney's drawing room, where he could talk of music among experts and had become a particular favourite of the family. All the Burneys, Fanny and Susanna included, were passionate supporters of Pacchierotti. Dr Burney roundly declared that he would knock down anyone who did not agree that his closes (cadenzas) were superior to those of any other singer, and Fanny and Susanna, with whom he loved to practice English, referred to him privately as their 'sweet Pacc.'.

There is no way of recapturing the sound of the castrato voice. The only recordings that exist were made in 1902 and 1904 by the last castrato at the Vatican, Alessandro Moreschi. The sound quality is poor, and Moreschi himself was past his prime, so that it is impossible to imagine from the faint, almost unearthly tones of the recording the delight, approaching ecstasy, that the castrato voice could inspire in eighteenth century audiences or the reasons which impelled so many great composers from Handel to Gluck and Mozart to write for it. When the great castrato Farinelli first appeared in London in 1734, a lady in the audience exclaimed 'One God, one Farinelli', a cry that was echoed through the opera house. Pacchierotti, Farinelli's successor as Europe's most famous castrato, was his equal in brilliance and virtuosity, but unlike Farinelli, who made no pretence at acting, Pacchierotti also excelled at conveying the fine shades of emotion. Lord Mount Edgcumbe, who described Pacchierotti in his musical reminiscences as the 'moſt perfeċt singer it ever fell to my lot to hear', wrote that 'the chief delight of his singing and his own supreme excellence lay in touching expression and exquisite pathos'. On one occasion in Rome, after Pacchierotti had sung a particularly moving passage of recitative due to be followed by an instrumental interlude, the orchestra stayed silent; when Pacchierotti turned inquiringly to the conductor, he was told by the weeping *maestro* that they were all in tears. On another, in London, the Duc d'Orléans (later Philippe Egalité) who never missed a performance by Pacchierotti when he was in England, arrived at the opera house with a large white handkerchief held ready in his hand; this started a fashion among the audience who for the rest of the season brought white handkerchiefs to all Pacchierotti's performances, raising them in unison whenever the royal visitor – clearly visible from his box – wiped his eyes.

For Dr Burney, Pacchierotti was quite simply the greatest singer of the age. In his *History of Music*, in which he devotes seven quarto pages to Pacchierotti, Burney describes his first impression of his singing. Pacchierotti was suffering from a cold, and singing only *sotto voce*; despite this, wrote Burney, his performance gave him more pleasure than anything he had ever heard before.

'The natural tone of his voice is so intereſting, sweet and pathetic, that when he had a long note, or *messa di voce*, I never wished him to change it, or do anything but swell, diminish, or prolong it in whatever way he pleased, to the utmoſt limit of his lungs. A great compass of voice downward, with an ascent up to B flat and sometimes to C, with an unbounded fancy, and a power not only of executing the moſt refined and difficult passages of other singers, but of inventing new embellishments, which as far as my musical reading and experience extended, had never then been put on paper, made him during his long residence here a new singer to me every time I heard him…When his voice was in order, and obedient to his will, there was a perfeċtion of tone, taſte, knowledge and sensibility, that my conception in the art could not imagine possible to be surpassed.'

Susanna Burney's letter-journals for the season of 1779-80 give us a vivid description of Pacchierotti's individual performances, but it is worth pausing for a moment to examine the whole phenomenon of the castrato voice, whose extraordinary power and sweetness was so much part of baroque music that any revival of it today, whether with a counter-tenor or soprano, can never quite recapture the composer's first intention. The practice of castration for musical purposes, either in opera or at church services, was at its height in late seventeenth and eighteenth century Italy, when the enormous salaries paid to top castrati made it a huge temptation to impoverished families to sacrifice a promising boy singer in the hope of making a fortune. Although strictly illegal, and usually presented as the result of a childhood accident rather than deliberate choice, it is estimated that at one point in the eighteenth century as many as 4,000 boys were castrated in Italy each year; very few, of course, made a fortune, though many found places in church choirs. Usually performed between the ages of seven and twelve, the operation involved the cutting of the spermatic cord leading from the testicles to the urethra; the testicles would then be removed, thus leaving the member permanently immature. It was generally carried out by putting the patient into a warm bath to soften the parts and make them more supple; after this the surgeon would dose him with opium, or press his jugular veins to make him insensible, and the action could be performed with almost no pain.

The vocal consequences of this mutilation went far beyond preserving the boy's treble voice into manhood. As he grew, so did the capacity of his lungs and chest, augmented by years of intensive training; it was not unusual for a castrato to be able to sustain a note for a full minute, something far beyond the capacity of most adult male or female singers. As well as vocal technique, the castrato would have learned to play the harpsichord and studied composition and counterpoint; the phenomenal ability of the great castrati to embellish, or improvise on, an aria was the result of a rigorous musical education. 'The mature castrato,' writes Henry Pleasants in his classic book, *The Great Singers*, 'was a boy soprano or alto with all the physical resources of a grown man, although, of course...with something missing.'

The 'something missing' made it impossible for castrati to procreate or make love fully. But it did not prevent them having love affairs; according to Byron, one of their great attractions for Italian women was that there was no risk of pregnancy. Pacchierotti himself had been involved in a duel with the lover of a Neapolitan marchesa who had fallen madly in love with him, though how much he responded to her adoration is uncertain.

Surprisingly none of the great castrati, whose voices won them so much fame and adulation, seem to have admitted to any deep sense of loss at their emasculation; in many cases, perhaps, the loss was sublimated in their art. For some listeners their sexual ambivalence merely added to their fascination. William Beckford, who arranged his Grand Tour around Pacchierotti's appearances in various Italian towns, described his singing as an incitement to forbidden (i.e. homosexual) passion: 'Such Musick – O Heaven it breathes the very soul of voluptuous effeminacy.'

Pacchierotti arrived in London in October 1779 to begin rehearsals for the coming season. Susanna's letter-journals to her sister re-open with a description of his first visit to St Martin's Street, accompanied by his friend and early teacher, the composer Ferdinando Gasparo Bertoni. 'Almost every great singer,' observed Dr Burney in his *History of Music*, 'unites himself in interest and friendship with some particular composer, who writes to his peculiar compass of voice, talents and style of singing'. Pacchierotti and Bertoni were thus closely connected, Bertoni acting as the house composer at the King's Theatre, Haymarket during Pacchierotti's London season.

'Wednesday Oct 20th,' writes Susanna, 'My aunt Nanny came to tea – in hopes she acknowledged that she should meet *with no foreigner*... However our tea things were not removed when we were alarmed by a rap at the door, and who should enter but *l'Imperatore del Canto* & his Treasurer – Pacchierotti & Bertoni – I beg you to guess who was charm'd and who looked blank – they wd. not drink any tea but seated themselves & stayed with us full three hours.'

Pacchierotti at this time was thirty-nine, tall and lanky – most castrati tended to be tall – with a thin, pale face which lit up with a look of inspiration when he sang. Proud and shy, he was usually rather silent in company, except with those, like the Burneys, with whom he felt at home. Then he expanded, talking freely in Italian or French, more haltingly in English, which he was passionately eager to learn. For Fanny, remembering him in old age, there was something poetic about his conversation: 'When he was highly animated...the effusions of his imagination resembled his cadences in music, by their extraordinary flights, and impassioned burſts of deep, yet tender sensibility'.

With Susanna on this occasion, he talked of the recent threat of invasion, then turned to the English books he had been reading. He read a few chapters of the Bible each day, he told her, and was finishing Lord Chesterfield's Letters and Hume's History of England. 'I ask'd him what Poetry he had read – a great deal of Pope's I found. He named *Windsor Foreſt* & *The Rape of the Lock*, & spoke of them in rapture but particularly the laſt.' He looked at the print of Dr Johnson which hung on the drawing room wall, and expressed 'the higheſt degree of respeҫt & veneration for the original, whose Diҫty. he intends to purchase.'

After asking when she expected Fanny home from Brighton – the following month, she told him – he mentioned having written her a note but was afraid that it was full of errors. '"Indeed…I am indeed a *truly Beaſt*" sd. he "My Memory is withered – faded". Impaired I told him was a better word – for wch. acquisition he thank'd me very much – he had before beg'd me to correҫt him when he sd. anything wrong…He made me wonderful fine speeches – & sd. at laſt "I am delightful to be in this company indeed…" but correҫted himself in a minute, & laughing added, "delighted I would say – Everything breathes – tout ici respire le scavoir – comment dit on cela?"…He asked me how he shd. say l'Ambassadeur de Naples in English – to make him underſtand Neapolitan I wrote it down – "Come scrive bene quella Creatura" sd. he caſting up his eyes to Bertoni – who joined in the Compliment…I sd. wch. was indeed true 'twas a vile pen – "Ah vous écrivez comme un ange" cried he – you'll excuse me – but I muſt write down Pacchierotti's compliments…If you had not written Evelina I would advise you to be jealous of me – As it is I am afraid I cannot occasion you any alarm.'

However much Susanna missed her sister it was a pleasure to have Pacchierotti to herself for a while, and her descriptions of their meetings, whether at home or seen through a crowd at rehearsals and performances, are the highlights of her letter-journals. She knew that her sister would share her interest in Pacchierotti, indeed preserved the fiction in her letters that it was Fanny, rather than herself, whom he most wished to see. The gallant Lieutenant Phillips, her future husband, was thousands of miles away and as yet unknown to her. There is no trace in her letters of anyone else who attracted her attention, though reading between the lines there were several – including the learned Italian Dr Baretti, translator of Dr Johnson's *Rasselas* – who may have wished to do so. Over the next few months it was Pacchierotti who absorbed her thoughts and emotions, other feelings swept aside in her ardent admiration for his singing. For someone so intensely musical as Susanna, there was nothing outrageously improbable about this; summing up the evidence of informed contemporary listeners, Henry Pleasants describes Pacchierotti as perhaps a greater artist even than Farinelli, quite possibly the greatest singer who ever lived.

As was the custom in most continental theatres, serious operas in England were sung in Italian, and most of the leading singers were Italian. The tradition harked back to the accession of George I, Handel's patron both in Hanover and London, to the throne in 1714. As the King understood Italian far better than English and was a passionate lover of opera, he had done much to encourage the taste for Italian opera among the nobility and gentry; a succession of operatic masterpieces by Handel had confirmed society's appetite for *opera seria* and made London a magnet for the leading castrati of the day. Since then, Italian opera had become an established part of musical life in London, with the King's Theatre, Haymarket, built by Vanbrugh at the beginning of the century, as its official home.

It remained an entertainment for the élite. The price of tickets and subscriptions for the King's Theatre was higher than in either of the two main theatres, and the audience was more exclusive: for many it was the wish to see and be seen by their fashionable friends, rather than the pure love of music which brought them there. Going to the opera was very much a social occasion, with gossip, refreshments and celebrity-watching as important parts of the evening's entertainment; since, as in every other theatre of the time, the auditorium remained fully lit during performances, it was easy to recognise acquaintances. There might be rapt attention when the castrato or the prima donna sang principal arias or duets, but the rest of the performance took place against a background of continual bustle and conversation.

In opera, it was the star singers, rather than the composers who drew the audiences, and though some of the leading composers of the day, including Gluck, Cherubini, J.C.Bach, and later Haydn, were engaged by the King's Theatre at various times, their works were freely altered or adapted as occasion and the voices of the singers demanded. The *pasticcio*, comprising a medley of arias by several different composers, set to a new or existing libretto, was a commonly accepted opera form, the leading singers often choosing the arias which best displayed their talents and, in the case of the castrati, inventing their own embellishments: the ideal was never to sing the same cadenza twice. A house composer, such as Bertoni, was often hard-put to coordinate the various elements of a *pasticcio*, nor was it clear whether he, the manager or the singers should have the final word.

For the King's Theatre during the season of 1779-80 the

question of who was in authority was especially uncertain. A year and a half before the opera company had been taken over by Richard Brinsley Sheridan and Thomas Harris, the principal owners and managers of Drury Lane and Covent Garden respectively. The two theatres already had the monopoly of spoken drama in London; by acquiring the King's Theatre, they controlled the main venue for Italian opera as well. (Ballad operas or burlettas in English, combining songs with spoken dialogue, were already a regular feature at Drury Lane and Covent Garden; Sheridan's *The Duenna*, with music by his father-in-law Thomas Linley, had been a huge success four years before.) Both partners hoped to make a quick profit, but whereas Harris was tight fisted and prudent, Sheridan was notoriously feckless and their first season had ended in a loss. By the summer of 1779 Harris, having had enough of his unreliable partner, handed over responsibility for their debts and the future running of the enterprise to Sheridan in exchange for his share of the ownership. Sheridan himself had no experience of music, though his wife, the former Elizabeth Linley, had been a celebrated soprano before her marriage; in any case he was too busy to run the opera house himself. His brilliant career as a playwright had reached its culmination with *The Critic*, first performed at Drury Lane that autumn, and his eyes were already set on entering Parliament. Distracted by politics, social life and the affairs of Drury Lane, he regarded the King's Theatre chiefly as a source of income and had engaged a would-be impresario, Antoine Le Texier, as a general administrator. It had been Le Texier who had engaged Pacchierotti and Bertoni, as well as the leading soprano Madame Le Brun.

Susanna, always interested in opera gossip, was amused to hear her father and the Italian tenor Gabriele Piozzi 'cutting up Mr Tessier very notably' in St Martin's Street one evening: in order to attract subscribers, Le Texier had simply made up a list of famous composers who he claimed had been engaged. 'I suppose you have seen Tessier's impudent puff in the Morng. Post where he names 7 or 8 Composers for the Opera this season, out of which number *but one* has been engaged by the Managers. – He begins wth. Sacchini, who has nothing to do this year – then Bertoni, who alone is engaged – he adds *Bach*, who is at Paris, Paisiello, in *Russia*, & 3 or 4 more.'

Pacchierotti had his own troubles with Le Texier. The first opera of the season was to have been a comic pasticcio, *Il Soldano Generoso*. Bertoni had arranged the music and Pacchierotti already learned his part when Le Texier announced that only three of the comic performers had arrived and the opera had to be changed at the last minute. 'I exclaimed against the management –' wrote Susanna, 'and indeed it is abominable as Pacchierotti says his head is now full of the *Soldano Generoso* wch. Bertoni has been made to compose for nothing.'

A new pasticcio, *Alessandro nell'Indie*, based on a text by the famous Italian poet and librettist Metastasio, was to take the place of the abandoned opera. With only fourteen days between the change of plan and the first performance, Bertoni worked frantically at putting the opera together; inevitably, the majority of songs were not his own, and most of those that were had already been used elsewhere. Pacchierotti, also under pressure, was to play the starring role. Susanna, who had read the libretto and shared Pacchierotti's annoyance with Le Texier, took a lively interest in their progress. On November 19, with her sister Esther and Esther's husband, she went to the general rehearsal at the opera house, 'a little *en tremblant*' at first but soon reassured by their civil reception at the mention of her father's name.

V

The rehearsal had already begun when Susanna and her sister and brother-in-law took their places towards the back of the pit. The theatre was half empty, with only two boxes occupied, one by two ladies Susanna did not know, the other by Lady Mary Duncan, well known for her adoration of Pacchierotti: William Beckford described her as being 'more preciously fond [of him] than a she bear of her suckling.'

Susanna found the opera disappointing on the whole, though she was charmed by Pacchierotti's singing of a cavatina *Se mai piu saro geloso* in the first act. 'It is Elegant, charming Music & admits of all those refinements and graces in which Pacchierotti so particularly excells – & He *did* sing it like a very Angel – to You it will give little trouble to conceive the pleasure I felt at hearing his most Sweet Voice, & that in such sweet music – but I would not answer for the *conception* of scarce anybody else…As an opera, I confess I have heard few that seemed to me possessed of a smaller number of fine, or even of *pleasing* airs than the present Alessandro…'

Cramer, the leader of the orchestra, was in trouble with his players. 'He is a charming *Creature* – so mild, so Gentlemanlike in his manner of speaking to the Band, at the same time it is evident he quite suffers when anything goes wrong – the Wind instruments were all out of tune, & tho' I pitied poor Cramer 'twas impossible not to laugh – After repeatedly desiring the French Horn players to make their instruments sharper, at last he called out in a voice wch. proved that he wth.difficulty cd. repress a degree of Indignation – & with his foreign accent – "Gentelmen [sic] – *you are not in tune At all." – "Its a very sharp morning, Sir"* sd. one of them – "We shall do better another time"…Presently after in another passage the Bassoon player was dreadfully and ridiculously out of tune…Pacchierotti, whose song was then playing then went and whispered something to Cramer, who in consequence of it, called to the Bassoon player by his name, & desired he *wd. omit playing the passage* – "Yes Sir – to be sure I will!" cried the Dolt, whose stupid, shameless Insensibility made everybody laugh, & in spite of his evident vexation Cramer at last, till he seemed almost choked by it.'

Le Texier came in at the end of the rehearsal and did not see the Burney party, as they were sitting in a dark place in the pit. 'I was not very miserable at this,' wrote Susanna, 'especially as the only Person I saw by whom I at all wished myself to be noticed was not long without observing me – this was – need I say Pacchierotti – We had approached the orchestra very gently during his Cavatina – presently after it the weather was so cold he gave *two or three jumps* to warm himself – during this performance he caught our eyes, & almoſt while he was yet *en l'air* took off his hat, laughing & bowing – "Il fait bien froid" sd. he to excuse his exhibitions I suppose, "très froid en verité". – As soon as the Duet wch. ends the Act was over, wch. is by the way preceded by some delightful recitative, I miss'd Pacchierotti on the ſtage & presently heard his voice behind me – "How does Miss Burney do?" sd. he, – "& Mr Burney & Mrs Burney? – all well I hope." Very happy to see & hear him again I told him.'

They settled down to a discussion of the opera, her brother-in-law criticising the duet, 'in doing which I found, as indeed *he* might have foreseen, He was in the wrong Box – Had Pacchierotti disliked it, certainly in a Paſticcio where there cd. be no obligation to do it, he wd. not have sung it – He sd. it was Piccini's laſt Composition – "*Une Musique* qui n'a pas été entendu encore – et belle en verité" & attributed Mr Burney's not liking it to it's having been ill executed but hoped Tuesday night it wd. go better…He asked me if I had heard the Cavatina – I sd. it was beautiful & beg'd to know the composer, but the noise of the inſtruments was so great I could not hear his answer – however he sd. of the music "Elle eſt charmante – il eſt vrai"…the next air was Piozzi's to wch. he *brava'd* away like anything – he told me 'twas Bertoni's song – In this pretty manner did he sit with us till recalled on ſtage to sing – & indeed the time he spent wth. us was more agreably pass'd by me than any other during which he was *not* singing.'

The next morning Cramer came to call, finding Susanna and her stepmother at breakfast – Dr Burney had already gone out. They talked at length about the opera and the difficulties of dealing with the management, above all with Sheridan himself. 'I have written three letters to Mr Sheridan at different times but have never recd. an answer,' he said. 'I have called 20 times, but never have been admitted – About half a year ago

I met him accidentally in the Street, & took the opportunity to speak to him – Very well, Mr Cramer – sd. he – But we can settle nothing here – Come & dine with me tomorrow & we will talk the matter over – Very well sir – at what o'clock – at four – accordingly the next day I went – I was shown upstairs & told Mr Sheridan was not yet home – well I waited till half an hour past *five*, a full hour & a half – but as nobody came near me & I was then *extremely hungry* I went away – & since that time I have never seen Mr Sheridan – & did he send me an apology – Never.'

This was typical of Sheridan's dealings with the opera company; devious and irresponsible, he was notoriously difficult to pin down. When he did intervene in the theatre's affairs, it was almost worse, for he seldom followed decisions through, and since he spoke little French and less Italian, communication with his leading artists was fraught with difficulties. In a scene from *The Critic*, surely based on his own experience, neither the interpreter nor the Italian singer Signor Pasticcio Ritornello can make themselves understood. The self appointed theatre expert, Mr Dangle, is at a loss:

> *Dangle*: Egad I think the Interpreter is the hardest to be understood of the two!
> *Sneer*: Why I thought Dangle you had been an admirable linguist!
> *Dangle*: So I am, if they would not talk so damn'd fast.

The Critic, first performed at Drury Lane on October 30, 1779, had been a resounding triumph for the author. The Duchess of Devonshire, who sat in Mrs Sheridan's box, was among the celebrities who attended the opening night. 'It is vastly good,' she wrote to her mother that same evening, 'it occasioned peals of laughter every minute.' Susanna and her parents had not yet seen it but Mrs Crewe, the fashionable beauty with whom Sheridan was said to be in love, had lent her manuscript copy of the play to Dr Burney. Susanna thought it could have been more graciously offered – 'She sent it by her Footman and consequently at the mercy of her servants' – but was delighted to have a chance of reading it.

The play was full of topical allusions, from the threatened invasion the previous summer –

> The Spanish fleet thou *canst* not see – because
> It is not yet in sight!

– to the Prime Minister Lord North, caricatured as the speechless Lord Burleigh. Even Sheridan has a mention. '*Writes himself!* I know he does,' says Sneer to a whispered aside from Sir Fretful Plagiary, who is afraid of plagiarism if he sends his play to Drury Lane: 'Why, Sir, for aught I know, he might take some of the best things in my tragedy and put them into his own comedy.'

The original of Sir Fretful Plagiary was said to be the playwright Richard Cumberland, successful enough in his own right but well known for his jealousy of other authors. Fanny had already experienced this characteristic when, at a party in Brighton with the Thrales, he had deliberately turned away when she was introduced to him. Fanny immediately moved off with Queeney Thrale, leaving Mrs Thrale to carry on the conversation. In the carriage on their way home Mrs Thrale described what had happened next.

'As soon as I made off,' Fanny told Susanna, 'he said in a *spiteful* tone of voice – "O, – that young lady is an Author, I hear!" – "Yes," answered Mrs Thrale, "Author of Evelina." "Hump, – I am told it has some humour" – "Ay indeed! – Johnson says nothing like it has appeared for years." "So! cried he, biting his lips, & waving uneasily in his Chair, – so! so!" – "Yes," continued she, – "& Sir Joshua Reynolds told Mr

Thrale he would give 50 pounds to know the Author." "So! so!
– O vaſtly well!" – cried he, putting his Hand on his Forehead.
– "Nay," added she, – "Burke himself sat up all Night to finish it!" – This seemed quite too much for him, – he put both
his Hands to his Face, & waving backwards & forwards, said
"O – vaſtly well – this will do for any thing!" – with a tone so
much as to say *pray no more!'*

Susanna was so indignant at Cumberland's conduct – 'So
mean – so illiberal – so obviously, glaringly little minded!'
– that she could not find it in herself to blame Sheridan for
his portrait of the envious Sir Fretful. 'No-one could miſtake
the Character who knows Mr Cumberland,' she was told by a
friend. 'His *son* found it out immediately – He is in the Guards
– I dined with him a few days ago and he cursed at Mr S. pretty
heartily.'

Fanny was due to return from Brighton with the Thrales
at the end of November. 'I hope she will pay you a visit,' said Dr
Baretti, when he called on the Burneys on November 22, 'tho'
now she has been exalted to the Thralic majeſty you muſt not
expect to see too much of her.' He had once been Italian tutor
to the Thrales and knew how demanding Mrs Thrale could be.

Baretti had arrived at St Martin's Street on a busy evening.
There was Mr Hutton, another family friend; the historical
painter, James Barry, currently engaged in painting a series of
six allegorical murals for the [Royal] Society of Arts; Susanna's
cousin Edward Francesco Burney, an aspiring young artist
much praised by Reynolds; Piozzi, the Italian tenor; Esther
and her husband as well as Dr Burney and his wife, and his
two younger daughters. It was a lively and amusing party, but
Susanna was too distracted to enjoy it. She had been hoping
that Pacchierotti would be coming, and between disappointment and uncertainty she could think of nothing else. It had
grown so late that she had given up all hopes of seeing him

when a knock at the door changed her mood in a moment: 'In came Pacchierotti & Bertoni – & the remainder of the evening was indeed passed most delightfully.'

Everyone greeted them with enthusiasm, Dr Burney especially rejoicing at seeing his favourite singer. Baretti appointed himself as master of ceremonies, seating Pacchierotti next to Esther and Susanna next to Bertoni (who spoke little English), bidding her talk Italian as fast as she could.

'"Ah! E brava quella Signorina" sd. Bertoni & many fine things – & when nobody attended I made out a little conversation with him – part French, part Italian…Pacchierotti now leaning over Bertoni with a smile asked me how his *Mistress* did & said to Baretti – "Miss Burney is so good as to be my *language* mistress." I declared incapacity – & had civil things sd. abundantly in consequence of doing so.'

Baretti then asked Susanna in low voice if Pacchierotti could not be persuaded to sing. 'If you will ask him,' said Susanna, who did not wish to press him. But Baretti, paying no attention to her scruples, turned to Pacchierotti and told him in Italian that Susanna had begged him to sing a song. '"Ah!" sd. he looking averse yet with great gentleness – & sd. he had lately sung himself almost to Death, it having been necessary for him to get an entire new part in twelve Days.'

Susanna then brought a copy of Bertoni's forthcoming pasticcio the *Olimpiade*, showing Bertoni the aria 'Superbo di mi stesso'. *'Ecco l'aria,'* she said, *'chi mi piace molto.' 'Brava,'* cried Baretti overhearing her. But Pacchierotti did not wish to sing and disappeared into a corner with her father to discuss a problem over 'a vile servant who has plagued him to death', and Baretti turned instead to her sister Esther (a professional musician before her marriage) to play the harpsichord.

'She played and extremely well indeed, a charming lesson in G of Emmanuel Bach's – before it was over Pac. joined the listeners and seemed greatly pleased with her playing…Baretti then renewed his attacks on Pacchierotti – I sd. I would find Music – "Trovera quella Signorina l'aria" sd. Bertoni laughing – "E quale?" sd. Pacchierotti to me – I showed him Superbo di mio Stesso. "Je ne peut pas chanter en verité" sd. he, & looked at me as if he hated to refuse tho' he was averse to complying with our requeſts – in return I cd. not bear to press.'

Everyone else however continued to plead for a song, Dr Burney finally suggesting that Pacchierotti should sing something less ambitious than the one Susanna had proposed. Pacchierotti however insisted on singing the music she had chosen, though he warned them he was not in voice.

'He sung this sweet [song] *Mezzo Bravura* – wch. I think altogether the prettieſt air of Bertoni I know…I never heard him so *well* in voice or in better Spirits – he was clear & in time – touching – perfeƈt – varied & improved all the divisions, & at a pause introduced in his song & in his *Cadenza* did *wonderful* things and wholly new – I never felt more exquisite delight in Music – Yet was he not satisfied – How would he sing I wonder!…He played all sort of tricks with his voice running up & down as high or low as he could – I knew his compass to be such that he could sing *Tenor* songs but I did not before *suspeƈt* he could vie with Agujari & Danzi [two well known sopranos] in their *alt-itudes* – will you believe me when I assure you, & with great truth, that in one of his runs he ran fairly up to the higheſt F of the Harpsichord…I could not help laughing & telling him that he wd. make Madame Le Brun jealous.'

After this there was more music, with Charles Rousseau Burney and his wife playing the harpsichord, and a further song by Pacchierotti, this time a rondo by Paisiello which he sang 'moſt angelically – with such infinite feeling and elegance that I cd. scarce keep the tears out of my eyes'. To Susanna's delight, he spent most of the rest of the evening talking to her. He rallied her on her diffidence about singing in company – 'Once – you remember… you was so good…we muſt have courage now' – and assured her that he himself was by nature the timidest person in the world. 'Some evening when Mr Bertoni and I have the pleasure to see you, you muſt do me the favour to sing to me…and if there are any little duets I shall be *infinitely* happy to sing them with you.' 'Now this you will allow was not a little *Soothing*…' wrote Susanna, 'I am sure I shd. have supposed he muſt have had enough of my singing – but he is all good Nature & politeness.'

Switching into French to express himself more freely, Pacchierotti went on to describe the difficulties of singing in Italian to an audience who for the most part did not understand it. If he took trouble to enunciate clearly no-one noticed, and if he tried to convey emotion in serious or dramatic moments he was merely accused of making grimaces. Only a handful of the fashionable public attending the theatre was truly capable of judging music; even then they were so fearful of making a *faux pas* that they waited for the verdict of an expert before giving their own, so that any spiteful critic had the power to ruin a singer. Luckily there were a few exceptions, among them Lady Clarges (an amateur musician and friend of Susanna's) and Susanna herself. 'Mademoiselle,' Pacchierotti said, turning to her sister, 'eſt capable de juger en *professeur*'. 'Doesn't your hair ſtand on end?' wrote Susanna at this tribute from the greatest singer of the age.

He complained of the intrigues and caballing he had met with in London. Even the *prima donna* Madame Le Brun, normally the most courteous of colleagues, had become capricious: in the first act of *Alessandro in Indie* in which Pacchierotti and Le Brun, as a jealous lover and his mistress, exchange vows and recriminations, it had been agreed that they should both sing arias by Piccini. 'You will readily conceive,' explained Susanna, 'that these two arias of the Duet should be the Composition of the same Master.' *'Eh bien,'* said Pacchierotti, 'on the morning of the rehearsal – without a single word to me – I was astonished to hear her sing a completely different aria, for which as you may have noticed her husband [the oboist] gave the key.' 'How injudiciously and wantonly ill bred and impertinent!' commented Susanna.

Pacchierotti repeated several times that had Madame Le Brun objected to the aria earlier he would not have minded – but to accept and then change it without the slightest explanation or apology showed a lack of consideration he had not expected. 'He attributed it however to her Husband I found, who is I believe an Insolent, disagreable man.' Susanna tried to console him by praising the recitative before the duet. 'And the duet is beautiful too, I assure you, if it is sung as it should be,' said Pacchierotti ruefully.

The evening broke up just after eleven, when Pacchierotti and Bertoni rose to go, the others following them soon after. It was only one of many such impromptu gatherings at Dr Burney's house, in which foreign celebrities and English musicians collaborated gladly, and which became a byword in the musical history of the time. A friendly caricature 'The Sunday Concert', printed two years later, depicts a somewhat similar evening: Lady Mary Duncan sits stiffly at one side; Bertoni is at the keyboard; Pacchierotti, with a sheet of music, leans forward next to him; the virtuoso oboist, Fischer, stands nearby. Meanwhile Dr Burney, always something of a ladies' man, is chatting intently in the corner to Mary Wilkes, the daughter of John Wilkes, her low cut dress revealing a formidable décolletage. Can it be that for once the great musicologist is not attending to the music?

VI

It was now three and a half years since Jem had left with Captain Cook's third expedition, and the family had heard no news of him since then. The idea of him tossing on unknown seas, in danger, perhaps even killed, must have been constantly in their minds. Dr Burney confessed later that he had almost given up hope of ever seeing his son again. Such thoughts put other concerns in perspective though Susanna's letter-journals, perhaps from a wish to avoid so painful a subject, make no mention of her worries for her brother. Instead she concentrates on what is close at hand, her most immediate anxiety that month the fact that Fanny had fallen ill at Streatham Park and her return to London had been delayed.

Mrs Thrale nursed Fanny herself, since her husband had been unwell and she did not wish to trouble the servants further. She was all sweetness in her bulletins to Fanny's family, but in the privacy of her journal she allowed herself to let off steam.

'Fanny Burney,' she wrote, 'has kept her Room here in my house seven Days with a Fever, or something that She called a Fever; I gave her every Medicine and every Slop with my own hand, took away her dirty Cups, Spoons &c. moved her Tables, in short was Doctor & Nurse, & Maid…and now – with the true Gratitude of a Wit, She tells me that the *World thinks the better of me* for my Civilities to her. It does! does it?'

It was evident that Fanny, for all her modest airs, was beginning to believe her own publicity. For Susanna, however, her sister could do no wrong. She was much too innocent to guess at Mrs Thrale's sharp comments or to be anything but grateful for her care. At a time when even the mildest illnesses were far more alarming than they are today, she was full of concern for Fanny and anxious to see her safely recovered. Meanwhile, Pacchierotti continued to be the theme of her letters, and she made much of his disappointment at not seeing Fanny. 'Your sister?' he asked Susanna as he made his way across the room towards her at a crowded gathering at St Martin's Street.

'"Oh! my sister", sd. I, turning up my eyes…I was unwilling to tell him that you were not well, as I knew it would seriously alarm & pain him…I therefore said somebody in the house where you were was not well – & that your friend Mrs Thrale had prevail'd on you to stay – "Indeed" – sd. he – "I am of your advice – I do not wonder – indeed – Miss Burney – she is such a charming Creature (clasping his hands) that they *would not* deserve so much pleasure if they did not desire to keep her."

'There's for you – you charming Creature! – then that I might not be jealous I believe – he said – "Indeed all the Sisters are so sensible – so charming that everywhere it must be they are desired!"'

It was another evening of music-making, with Cramer on the violin and Esther on the cello taking part in trios and quartets and the guest of honour, a Mr Pennech, purring after Charlotte 'like a big black cat'. Pacchierotti sat by Susanna while they played, and she had the pleasure of finding that they felt the same in the same places. Finally Pacchierotti was persuaded to sing, choosing the rondo by Paisiello that he had sung on the previous occasion at St Martin's Street. Cramer accompanied him on the piano, playing so divinely, wrote Susan, that it was even better than before.

'Pacchierotti did not *run riot* so much as when he sang

this sweet Roundeau to us before…but he evidently took more pains – & was so perfectly in tune and so touching in his expression that I cd. have worship'd him. When it was over I told him I had heard him sing this Rondeau as many times as I had fingers, wch. is I believe literally true, & that he was always new & seemed to me to sing it more perfectly every time I heard him. "Oh! cried he – Miss Burney is *so* encouraging to me – in everything – in Music, in language – Indeed if I was so happy to have many such hearers as you I believe I *would not perish!*" "No – nor ever will I hope"– cried I – & added laughing that he ought to be immortal. "Indeed, sd. he, if I could succeed always as I wish to do, I would merit your applause – but I am afraid sometimes, *that they are my intentions* which are only good.'" Susanna corrected his English, but the remark was characteristic of Pacchierotti. He had none of the vaingloriousness of most leading castrati; according to Lord Mount Edgcumbe, he was modest and diffident to a fault, remaining dissatisfied with himself even when he had given the greatest delight to his hearers.

Fanny arrived in London in mid-December, staying with her family but much in demand by Mrs Thrale, who did not intend to let go of her celebrated protegé, however irritating she sometimes found her. Her own family situation was difficult; her husband, who had recently suffered a minor stroke, was sluggish and lethargic, only to be roused from his inertia by flirting with the pretty young Sophie Streatfield, another member of her circle. Her eldest daughter Queeney, now fifteen, was sullen and hostile to her mother; Fanny, who got on well with Queeney, helped to lighten the atmosphere between them. Unable to resist the persuasions of Mrs Thrale, Fanny spent much of her time in Southwark, where the Thrales had a house next to the family brewery, or sallying forth with them on visits and shopping expeditions.

On most Sunday evenings the Thrales called at St Martin's Street, sometimes accompanied by Dr Johnson – the great man tending to fall asleep when there was music. Mrs Thrale herself, according to Fanny, had no feeling for music beyond what was fashionable, but she respected it nonetheless. Not only had she engaged Dr Burney, the most distinguished music teacher of the day, to teach Queeney, but she would later arrange for the handsome young tenor Gabriele Piozzi to give her daughter singing lessons too. Piozzi, whom she had first met with the Burneys, became a frequent visitor to Streatham Park in the summer of 1780, delighting even the phlegmatic Thrale with his singing and playing. Susanna's journals show him in a less attractive light. Although he had a fine voice himself, he was eaten up by jealousy of Pacchierotti, hating to applaud him or to hear him praised. This became so noticeable that Susanna did her best to sit well away from him whenever Pacchierotti was performing.

Even after her sister's return home Susanna continued her habit of journalising, retreating to the chilly refuge of the observatory to jot down her impressions. Her parents, who expected her to play her part in entertaining the stream of visitors to St Martin's Street, begrudged her the time she spent in writing and she had to snatch her moments when she could. The journal continues its daily record of small events; then, early in January, tucked away almost casually among her descriptions of evening visits and opera gossip, we suddenly come on a momentous two line entry:

'Wednesday, the 3rd of the month [January, 1780]…We had news of poor Capt. Cook's shocking death but at the same time of poor James's safety tho' no letters.'

The news must have reached them before the general public, perhaps through the kindness of Lord Sandwich, who had always taken a friendly interest in Jem. It was not until

January 11 that the official announcement appeared in the *London Gazette:*

'Captain Clerke of His Majesty's Sloop *Resolution,* in a letter to Mr Stephens, dated the 8th of June, 1779, in the Harbour of St Peter and St Paul, Kampschatka, which was received yesterday, gives the melancholy account of the celebrated Captain Cook, late commander of that Sloop, with four of his private Marines having been killed on the 14th of February last at the island of O'Why'he, one of a group of newly discovered Islands, in the 22nd Degree of North Latitude, in an affray with a numerous and tumultuous Body of Natives.'

The news spread through England, causing universal grief; perhaps only with the death of Nelson, more than a quarter of a century later, was the loss of a national hero felt so deeply. Zoffany's famous painting of Cook's last moments, exhibited at the Royal Academy the following year, helped confirm the mythic status of the man whose achievements, in the words of one obituary, were 'an everlasting honour to his country'. Three years later Cook's eagerly awaited journals of the voyage were published in three volumes with engravings from the paintings of John Webber, a young Swiss artist who had accompanied the expedition. Webber's dramatic, but probably more factual, painting of Cook's death gave Molesworth Phillips his moment of immortality. He is shown in the foreground, knocked down to a sitting position but still firing vainly at the man who is stabbing Cook.

Susanna's journal gives no account of her family's reactions to Cook's death or the welcome fact that Jem was safe, perhaps because Fanny, her usual confidante, was there beside her. But Fanny in one of her chatty letters to Mr Crisp expands a little further. 'I'm sure you must have grieved for poor Captain Cook,' she writes on January 22. 'How hard, after so many dangers, so much toil – to die in so shocking a manner – in an island he had himself discovered – among savages he had himself, in his firſt visit to them, civilised and rendered kind and hospitable, and in pursuit of obtaining juſtice in a cause in which he himself had no intereſt but zeal for his other captain!'

She gave him what news she had of her brother:

'Now concerning Admiral Jem – you have had all the accounts of him from my mother; whether he has made any change in his situation we cannot tell. The *Morning Poſt* had yeſterday this paragraph:

'"We hear Lieutenant Burney has succeeded to the command of Capt. Clerke's ship."

'That this, as Miss Waldron said of her hair, is all a falsity, we are however, certain, as Lord Sandwich has informed my father that the firſt lieutenant [King] of poor Capt. Cook was promoted to the Discovery. Whether however, Jem has been made firſt lieutenant of the Resolution, or whether that vacancy has been filled up by the second lieutenant of that ship [Williamson] we are not informed.'

In fact as we know, Jem had been made first lieutenant of Cook's former ship, a more important position than that he had held under Clerke, while Williamson had taken his place on the smaller *Discovery*. Phillips and his marines were on board the *Resolution* – perhaps just as well since the simmering hatred between him and Williamson showed no signs of abating. Phillips's friendship with Jem on the other hand was strengthened by the fact that they were both on the same ship. They had much in common. Like Susanna, Phillips was passionately fond of music and the theatre: he played the violin in shipboard concerts (with Jem as the musical director) and had once pawned his shirt to hear one of Garrick's last performances. Bluff and breezy, with a generous share of Irish charm, he had pretensions to gentility. His father was the natural son of the first Viscount Molesworth, a wealthy Dublin merchant and landowner, and Phillips stood – or so he hoped – to inherit some of his property in Ireland. Like Jem, he was adventurous and resourceful; their joint experiences of danger and hardship formed an emotional bond, perhaps similar to that of those who have served in war together, which remained untouched by later family rifts.

On January 13, 1780, just as the news of Cook's death reached England, the *Resolution* and the *Discovery* left Macao and started on their long voyage home. As well as re-fitting and re-clothing the crew, whose clothes had been literally in rags, they had taken on extra guns in view of the fact that Britain was at war. They had reason to hope their precautions would be unnecessary. Shortly before leaving they had heard news from Canton that out of regard for Cook and his achievements the respective governments of France and America had issued instructions that they were not to be molested; this news was confirmed by other ships they met on the way home.

Secure in the 'generosity of our enemies', as King expressed it, the two ships had an uneventful journey to the Cape, where they learnt that Spain too had entered the war but had also ordered their immunity. They were greeted with every kind of civility and attention by the governor and local officials, who knew Cook well from previous visits and heard the news of his death with genuine sorrow. Only one untoward incident marred their stay, when Williamson, meeting Phillips in the Assembly Room at Capetown, suddenly drew his sword and ran at him. Phillips, who was unarmed, avoided the thrust and, snatching a sword from the scabbard of someone who was standing near him, managed to disarm his assailant and would have taken the fight further if the company round him had not intervened. It was a murderous and unprovoked attack, which might well have ended fatally, and though King makes no mention of the incident in his official journal, it must have added greatly to the tensions of the homeward voyage. Surprisingly Williamson was not censured for his behaviour either then or at the time of Cook's death. Nor were his chances of promotion spoiled, while the more deserving Jem spent long periods of the next few years ashore. Williamson finally met his come-uppance as captain of the *Agincourt* at the battle of Camperdown in 1797 when, in an incident recalling his failure to come to Cook's help, he refused to engage the enemy despite signals instructing him to do so and was court-martialled for cowardice and disaffection. The charges were later changed to negligence, but they effectively put an end to his career.

On May 9, after a month spent refitting and taking on stores, the *Resolution* and the *Discovery* set out on the last leg of their journey. Every one was now desperately impatient to get home, infuriated by the Atlantic storms and calms which delayed them. On August 12 they reached the west coast of Ireland and, after a fruitless attempt to get into Galway Bay, were forced to steer northwards by strong southerly winds. It was not until August 22 that both ships came to anchor at Stromness on Lewis Island. From there Gore sent King overland to inform the Admiralty of their arrival in home waters, and Jem took command of the *Discovery*. After waiting more than a month in Stromness for a favourable wind, they at last made their way down the east coast and anchored at Yarmouth on September 30. On October 6 the ships dropped anchor at Deptford, their final destination. After an absence of four years, two months and twenty two days, Cook's last expedition was at an end.

Jem, it seems, wrote no letters to his family from the Cape, much to his sisters' disgust. 'Mr Jem,' complained Fanny, 'has not written one line.' But there was news to be gleaned from those connected with the navy, and there are various references to the expedition in Fanny's journals. In February, for instance, she meets the famous naturalist Dr Solander, who had travelled with Cook on his first voyage and whose descriptions of Kamchatka, which he visited then, would have been very close to Jem's experiences. On another occasion, when a certain Lord Mulgrave makes a joke about the roughness of naval manners, she cannot help reddening in Jem's defence. 'Poor Jem,' she wrote, 'God send him back safe, polished or rough.' And in July she reports that George III, who was said to have shed tears at Cook's death, had received Cook's journals, which he had asked to be the first to read.

Thanks to her friendship with Mrs Thrale, Fanny moved in a far more varied (though not necessarily more interesting) circle than her sister and was more likely to be in touch with the latest gossip, whether it be of Cook's voyages or current affairs in general. Susanna's journals, by contrast, remained concerned almost exclusively with musical matters, above all the encounters with Pacchierotti which were becoming more and more her reason for keeping them. During the months that Jem and her future husband were making their way home, we return to her world of the drawing room and opera house, a thousand miles away, both literally and metaphorically, from the hardships and dangers of shipboard life.

VII

Fanny was visiting the Thrales when Pacchierotti and Bertoni came to call at St Martin's Street on Wednesday, January 13. They had arrived after the first rehearsal of Bertoni's new opera *Quinto Fabio,* his first major opera to be performed in London. Susanna asked when the next rehearsal would be. "'You should come Miss Burney!'" said Pacchierotti 'so sweetly I shall never forget it', and promised that he would let her know the day. On the following Wednesday he sent her 'a very pretty note' telling her there would be a rehearsal the next morning, and a further, final one on Friday.

'I had then so bad a cold that I could not go –' she wrote, 'Fanny being likewise engaged to dine in the Borough [with the Thrales] I therefore wrote an answer telling my piteous case to Pacchierotti.' The next evening, while she was having tea with Sally and Patty Payne, the two pretty daughters of the publisher Thomas Payne, 'sweet Pacchierotti' came to enquire after her cold. For once Bertoni was not with him – he was putting the finishing touches to the overture. When the Paynes, 'whom he admired very much' had left, he read Susanna some of his favourite scenes from the forthcoming opera.

Susanna had her reservations about Bertoni's work, finding it at times derivative: she described one aria, for instance, as '*Strongly* in Sacchini's manner – rather too much, not for the song but the Composer.' She may well have agreed with her father that Bertoni's operas, though graceful and pleasing, perhaps lacked 'sufficient genius and fire to attain the sublime'.

But *Quinto Fabio*, which had already been a triumph in Milan, was one of his most successful works, and the story, based on the quarrel of the Roman general Quinto Fabio with his father-in-law, the emperor, whose orders he had disobeyed in battle, was full of dramatic possibilities.

'I like the Drama very much indeed,' wrote Susanna, '& if the Italian language was better underſtood, I doubt not that it wd. add very much to the success of the Opera – particularly as Pacchierotti feels every word of his part, & will give it all the expression it admits of – indeed he is full of intelligence... I told him I hoped not withſtanding my cold to be able to come next Morng. to the Opera House to hear Quinto Fabbio rehearsed. "Oh," cried he, "You muſt not *hasarde* yourself – it will be too cold."'

On Friday however she did *hasarde* herself and felt herself very well repaid:

'Quinto Fabbio is a charming opera & infinitely superior to anything I have heard of Bertoni's since he arrived in England... In the 2nd aĉt he [Pacchierotti] has a great Air which contains, I believe, 5 different movements – It begins Majeſtically – then breaks out wth vehemence – falls into a Cantabile "Sposa, tu piangi!" & returns I think to the firſt subjeĉt, & ends as an Aria Parlante full of Passion. – 'Tis a very fine & difficult song, & Pacchierotti exerts himself in it amazingly – & is so delicious in the slow part that I am dying for him to have a Cantabile throughout...What can be his objection – it exhauſts him too much I believe.'

She had gone to the rehearsal with Esther and Fanny. They sat close to the orchestra, where the 'agreable Cramer' greeted them, and Bertoni looked up from the harpsichord to ask Susanna how she was. Pacchierotti smiled and bowed on seeing them but could not make his way across the crowded pit to join them. He had been talking to Lady Edgecumbe, one of the great musical patrons of the day, and Susanna saw her asking him who they were.

It was only in public places, as opposed to their private meetings, that Susanna realised how sought after Pacchierotti was. A whole coterie of fashionable music lovers had made him their idol; in a period when the aristocracy were still the leaders of opinion, even Pacchierotti could not afford to ignore them. There was Lady Mary Duncan, who was said, quite inaccurately, to have given him a large sum of money; later that season she was forced to buy up the entire impression of a ludicrous caricature of herself and Pacchierotti in order to prevent a scandal. There were the three Bull sisters, all aspiring amateur singers. 'Oh how the Miss Bulls do idolise him!' wrote Fanny. 'They profess thinking him quite angelic, and declare they should even look upon it as a favour to be beat by him!' There were the Burneys' old friends, Lady Hales and Mrs Castle, both assiduous followers of the opera, and Susanna's special friend and patron, the beautiful Lady Clarges. 'I really love Lady Clarges,' wrote Susanna, '& she is to *me* always everything I could wish.'

A fine singer and harpsichordist who had studied with the great castrato singer Millico, Lady Clarges enjoyed playing and discussing music with Susanna and loved to share her enthusiasm for Pacchierotti with her. 'Huzza, huzza, I am so happy,' she wrote when he first came to England. 'Pacchierotti is arrived safe, sweet creature!…Pray, pray, my dear sweet Miss Burney *persuade* him to make me a visit next month.' Since then she had seen much of him in London and, like Susanna, tried to teach him English. But she spoke so fast, and used so much fashionable slang, that he was often puzzled. One day she told him that he had 'cut her' at some party. *'Come! vi taglio?'* he asked bewildered.

On Saturday evening, January 22, Susanna and Fanny

attended the premiere of *Quinto Fabio*. It was received with great applause she wrote, despite hissing from 'some spiteful wretches' in the gallery during one of Pacchierotti's encores. Susanna was in a fever on his behalf, 'but the violence of the applause and encores increased in proportion to the resistance they met – poor Pacchierotti's voice faultered sadly at first however he grew steadier by degrees and ended the rondo divinely.'

They had much talk on the subject later. 'I find he attributes it to some personal enemies who take advantage of his being encored to vent their spite – "I have not been *accustomed* to it indeed" – I sincerely hoped he never would be but this Barbarous abominable practice quite defeats him, & makes him dread to be encored.'

This was only one of Pacchierotti's troubles. Already he was beginning to experience the difficulties of dealing with Sheridan. 'He complained much of the ill management of the Opera House – sd. he had never performed in a Theatre so vilely out of repair, that it was a *Republic* as Mr Sheridan wd. not act, & there was no chief – that the lowest of the Performers behaved with such insolence that Bertoni dared not speak to them even when they were singing his music.' Pacchierotti had found the same and had been treated so rudely by the other singers when he asked them to look at him or approach him as the drama demanded, that, knowing he would not be master of himself if he once responded, he was reduced to silence.

Nor were Sheridan's financial dealings straightforward. For instance he had made Pacchierotti a verbal offer (probably concerning extra performances), then written a fulsome letter confirming it, which turned out to be for only half the sum proposed. Pacchierotti was a gentle, unassuming man, but he knew his own value and had not been at the top of his profession for nearly twenty years for nothing. He sent Sheridan an excellent letter, wrote Susanna, 'to say he was no longer a little boy satisfied with sugar plumbs, & that the smoke from the incense pot wd. not do alone &c. &c., since wch. he has heard no more of the manager in queſtion.'

Despite these irritations there were moments of glory which made up for all. On March 9, Susanna, Fanny and Charlotte went to hear Pacchierotti in his benefit performance (in which the evening's proceeds went to him) of the *Olimpiade*, a *pasticcio* by Bertoni, based on a drama by Metastasio. The audience, which included Sir Joshua Reynolds, the Duke of Dorset and the Duchess of Devonshire as well as Pacchierotti's usual devotees, was a brilliant one, and the house was crowded to the ceiling.

'The opera went off extremely well & gave me infinite pleasure,' wrote Susanna. 'Made Le Brun was feebly applauded indeed, even in her great song – but 'twas no wonder, for the house was full of Pacchierotti's friends and those who feel all *his* excellences. She can never charm...but Pacchierotti – Oh! Pacchierotti – how divine he was!...In his great scene *Misero! Che veggo* &c. between the Drama – the Composition & his performance I was – absolutely melted – & cried as I did at the firſt serious opera I heard – I never heard anything more touching nor shall ever recolleċt it without emotion...It was felt by the Audience wonderfully...No – not wonderfully since it was felt only as it ought to be – such a murmur spread especially from that corner of the Pitt where my Father sat, of whispered bravos, as I scarce ever heard – & the moment, nay even *before* the song was quite done there was a burſt of vehement applause... The Rondo in the laſt aċt *Ti seguiro fidele* was I believe never so sung before – often as I have heard it I never heard Pacchierotti so perfeċt in it as this night – it was encored with fury & he repeated it in a manner which was wholly new – moſt divinely indeed – & it was so applauded, that the scene was changed, & he upon it again before the audience could ſtop their hands.

'When all was over he came forward with the usual ceremonies to bow – there was such applause as I scarce ever remember – he bowed, & bowed, & bowed again & cd. scarce get away – the colour rose in his face, & I really believe 'twould have been a relief to him to have cried – I cd. have cried myself with pleasure & perturbation. He cd. hardly get away – yet had he not at laſt retired, the applause for ought I know might have laſted till *now*, & nobody seemed inclined to give up.'

In the middle of the third act, while he was standing at the side of the stage, Pacchierotti saw the Burney party and smiled and bowed to them. 'After this,' wrote Susanna, 'he had no reſt, as everybody was curtsying to him, even when he was on the ſtage, wch. I saw embarrassed even whilſt it flattered him.' When the opera was over her father went up to him. He seemed very happy, she wrote, and said the reception he had met with from so many friends that evening meant more to him than any financial gain could ever do. 'For my part,' she concluded, 'I have not been so happy for a great while as I was this night.'

Four days later, Susanna was able to congratulate him in person, when they met at the Pantheon in Oxford Street, where she had gone to hear a concert with her sisters and her brother in law, Dr Burney joining them from time to time. A centre for concerts, ridottos and assemblies, the Pantheon consisted of a large domed central rotunda (said to be based on Santa Sophia in Constantinople) with a series of smaller reception rooms for cards and suppers leading off it. During the interval they saw Pacchierotti among the crowd in the rotunda; he bowed to Susanna with 'a mighty pleas'd look' and later joined them after the concert. The suggestion had been their father's. 'Dr Burney, he tell me you desire my company at tea?' he said, coming up to them as they waited to go to the tea room downstairs.

"'Yes indeed" sd. Fanny and I *together* I believe, "if you can come" "Oh Ma'am I am very happy" – accordingly we went to the Regions below together – & Fanny and I repeatedly told him how delighted we had been at his Benefit, with his singing & the reception he had met with. "Indeed" sd. he, "the pleasure to me was very great…I am very sensible – very grateful, indeed to the goodness that was shown to me on that occasion."'

They stood a long while waiting for seats in the tea room, the other members of their party, Charlotte, Esther and her husband, finding places before them. Finally, just as their father came up, they found a table to themselves, where Susanna and Fanny 'nursed up' Pacchierotti very nicely. 'I thought he would prefer coffee to tea and called to Papa – "Papa" repeated he – "Ah Casa" – indeed he has quite an affection for our family & seems always delighted at seeing us affectionate to each other – but when *Papa* had got in the coffee it proved thick & good for nothing – "It is" sd. he, "just like some stuff Lady Clarges pour'd out for me at Ly Archer's last night, & I said to her *Ma'am* you have *empoison'd me*" – he beg'd some tea of me to take the taste out of his mouth – I said I was sorry he fared so ill & that the Coffee was so nasty. "Oh" sd. he, "Your company proves the antidote" – & several more such pretty speeches…He was as good humour'd & seemed as happy as we cd. wish him. I half *scolded* my Father for hurrying us from the table before I had finished my cup of tea tho' the truth was I had dawdled at it only to bear him company.'

On the way from the tea room they met Lady Clarges with her sister-in-law and two friends. 'I believe she envied us having Pacchierotti,' recorded Susanna with satisfaction, all the more so since Pacchierotti stayed with them till the end of the evening, even though they had seats and he was forced to remain standing. Lonely through circumstance, with no boon companion but Bertoni, he seemed to find especial pleasure in the Burneys' company. 'He wished over & over again that he was of our Family!' wrote Susanna on another occasion, '...Bertoni in Italian sd. to me that there were families, one in particular he mentioned in Venice, who were all musical – others like the Bourbon family (NB according to *him* not me) all *Fools* – & few shine like Dr Burney's family where all abounded in talents & all were cultivated & intelligent.' 'Very preti!' she concluded.

Mrs Thrale, despite her love for Fanny, did not always appreciate this atmosphere of Burney worship. There was an element of class feeling in her attitude. 'The Burneys are I believe a very low race of Mortals,' she once confided in her diary. But this was only a fleeting lapse. Dr Burney, cultivated, easy, charming, a favourite with Dr Johnson, was now an established member of her circle. His portrait was the most recent of the famous collection which the Thrales commissioned Reynolds to paint of their family and friends. Dressed in his robes as a Doctor of Music, he would hang in the drawing room at Streatham, together with such luminaries as Johnson, Burke, Garrick, and Reynolds himself. In the end the aristocracy of talent had special claims. Meanwhile Mr Thrale, who had recently suffered another small stroke, was still jaded and unwell, and she hoped to cheer him with a change of scene, this time a trip to Bath. Fanny, of course, was expected to go with her – 'I can't do without her and there's an end,' she told Dr Burney – and on March 28 the Thrales, accompanied by Sophie Streatfield, spent a farewell evening at St Martin's Street.

Pacchierotti arrived soon after them, a little overwhelmed by so much company at first but soon settling down to talk with

Susanna. Mrs Thrale, in general, had no liking for such 'beings'; unlike the Burneys, steeped in music, she saw a castrato as a freak or oddity. But she had taken a fancy to Pacchierotti on her earlier visits there, finding him elegant, humble and gentle, with a surprising adroitness in languages – his progress in English, she considered, was astonishing. 'As for his singing,' she concluded, 'I understand it not, but the best Judges say it is exquisite, & Basta cosi.'

Queeney Thrale came up to talk to Susanna, giving her her hand very cordially but refusing to sit down. 'She is very much your good friend,' said Pacchierotti when she had gone. 'Ye-es,' said Susanna a little doubtfully.

'And Mrs Thrale also?'

'They are very good – but *Fanny* is their particular friend and favourite.'

'Very true – but you likewise.'

'Oh – for her sake I believe they like me well enough.'

'NO – for yourself,' insisted Pacchierotti. 'Indeed – you merit it – but there is a difference in your friends I think. This family [the Thrales] they are so attached to Miss Fanny – and Lady Clarges she seem to me to love you better than all the rest.'

'Oh – she knows me better.'

'Oh, but many people I see do – there is a division – different tastes – but for me,' he concluded triumphantly, 'I am indeed for both!'

The Thrales and Fanny left together to spend the night at Southwark before setting off the next day. 'The Moment of your Departure,' wrote Susanna to Fanny, 'was to me & indeed to all, a very unpleasant one – it really produced the effect of annihilating at the time even the recollection that the rest of the eveg. had been delightfully spent…I did not see half enough of you – nor speak to you, nor embrace you when you went as I wanted to do – & yet 'twas silly to make a fuss for such a journey as this too – one wch. promises to afford you great pleasure, without either fatigue or danger, & is not to be of endless duration. Well! When the carriage had driven off, I ran up ſtairs & buſtled into the room with Dr Gillies & Charlotte – I was a little fluſtered but found the fair S.S. [Sophie Streatfield] with the tears yet gliſtening in her eyes.'

Susanna did not take Sophie Streatfield's tears at losing the Thrales too seriously – she was well known among her friends for her ability to cry becomingly at will. 'But Pacchierotti …Pacchierotti's eyes were in juſt the same ſtate, partly owing to his own concern at your departure, partly to his soft & gentle disposition wch. was moved by the beautiful sight SS presented to his view – as he had no previous knowledge of her he could not but be touched at such a display of her sensibility.'

He made way for Susanna on the sofa, then took a place next to her. He would insist, she wrote, that she should cry as well, but she assured him with great truth that she never did such things in public. After this he talked on for a while, but for once she was not listening. 'You are very absent,' he said smiling. Susanna could not disagree. 'Oh!' he said, 'you have a very sensible soul – I am sure of it. It seems to me that you are particularly attached to Miss Fanny – & she to you – More than the reſt – there seems but one soul – but *one mind between you* – you are two in one.'

Susanna did not deny it but assured him that she did not find their parting especially painful, since Fanny was travelling with a family she loved and she would soon be seeing her again. This led Pacchierotti to think about his own departure, for he would be leaving London at the end of the season in early July, and to the chagrin of his many devotees he had made no engagement for the following year.

'I must cry,' he said, 'I am sure very much when I leave behind England – And it will be the first time I shall have cried on such an occasion – It will be like the grief of *a man who loses his mistress…I* have no mistress but indeed the English people please me *particularly…* They all seem good to me – but most especially the *women…* indeed it appears so to me – *I am not in the way* to assure myself of it by nearer speculation – you know – indeed only by *transitory observations…*'

Susanna felt they were getting into deep waters. 'I was not sorry to have an end put to this speech of poor Pacchierotti's, as I knew not where it might lead him – I am afraid he wishes he cd. marry.'

She changed the subject to suggest that he should write to Fanny while she was away. 'You must *encourage* me then,' he said. 'Oh you need no encouragement in this case I think,' said Susanna; 'however I will take care to send the letter if you will write it.' Pacchierotti insisted that he would only do so if he could ask her for advice in writing it. 'I wish he may keep his word,' wrote Susanna, as he left her with a promise that he would soon be troubling her again.

VIII

Plunged into a round of expeditions, plays and evening visits, Fanny had barely a moment to herself in Bath. But her time was not wasted, for in the words of her old mentor, Samuel Crisp, she was now at 'the great school of the world', where swarms of new ideas and characters presented themselves and she could begin to think of her next novel. Susanna's letters from St Martin's Street kept her in touch with all that was going on at home, though in the teeth of their stepmother's disapproval. 'The worst of it is that somebody else is much sour'd when she discovers me to be thus employed – so that I am obliged to steal time & suffer cold in order to escape observation,' wrote Susanna. Once again, the draughty observatory, from which Sir Isaac Newton had observed the heavens, was a refuge from the family's demands.

Susanna's first news after Fanny's departure was that Pacchierotti had been very ill. She had sent round a note to his lodgings in Soho Square, wishing him a speedy recovery in the name of their family, which William, their manservant, had great difficulty in delivering since Pacchierotti's entrance was crowded with well wishers on the same errand. She did not see him again till April 12, when she attended a rehearsal of Sacchini's opera *Rinaldo* and found him looking sadly ill – 'as thin as possible, and paled and sallow'. Three or four times he made his way towards her with smiling eyes but was hooked each time by some importunate claimant so that she had no chance to talk with him. The next day, however, she was alone with Charlotte drinking tea when they were alarmed by a loud knock on the door.

'We had agreed to be denied,' she wrote, 'however something came cross my mind & I ran to the door to liſten – "I believe, Miss" sd. Willm., before he open'd the door, "it is Mr Pacchierotti's carriage" – I need not tell you what my orders were in that case – & so it proved – in a minute Pacchierotti entered – Lord – I was so glad!'

She told him how pleased she was to see him looking better and how she had tried in vain to talk to him at the rehearsal. 'Oh, I was much mortified,' he said, 'indeed I tried several times to approach you – but I was always ſtopt by Lady Clarges, Miss Bulls…'

They talked of Sacchini's opera, Pacchierotti complaining that he made him sing 'like a grasshopper', and of his latest problems with the proprietor.

'Mr Sheridan he use me very ill,' he said, 'I assure you I have a great will…*come si dice* – a great mind to call him Rascal. He provoke me too much! Laſt night at the Opera House, he told me he wanted very much to speak to me, & beg'd of me to call on him at 12 today – At twelve accordingly, & I was very exaɕt, I called on him – he was not at home but the servant said me however that he was sorry to disappoint me, but wd. call on me certainly between 4 & 9 this evening…'

'Have you seen him then?' asked Susanna.

'*Me?* No…Indeed he seem to behave so for the purpose to affront me – I will write to him a note.'

And taking a paper from his pocket, Pacchierotti proceeded to write the following lines:

'Pacchierotti sends his Comps. to Mr Sheridan, & is very displeased to be oblig'd to call him a Rascal, but his conduɕt is in everything so irregular he can give no better title to so great a Breaker of his word, wch. I wish it may bring him to the gallows.'

He then drew a picture of a gallows, with a man hanging from it and himself at the bottom pulling down his legs.

'Did you ever hear the like!' asked Susanna. 'You will be shocked – but had you been of the party you muſt have laugh'd – & Pacchierotti vowed he wd. send it tomorrow by wch. he at laſt half frightened me – however he ended by saying that he was not capable to send anybody such an Insult, & when they met shd. perhaps scarce reproach him for his breach of word.'

Sacchini's *Rinaldo* was musically the most important opera of the season. One of the most famous and popular composers of the time, Sacchini was a close friend of the Burneys and like Pacchierotti greatly respected Susanna's musical judgement. She had been flattered when, meeting him at the rehearsal, he had asked her if she had liked the work. 'More than I can say', she told him truthfully. *'Mais réelement?'* asked Sacchini, *'parceque votre opinion je l'eſtime en verité plus que tous les compliments qu'on a le bonté de me faire. Etes vous contente?'* Susanna repeated her praises. *'Eh bien,'* said Sacchini, *'Vous me ferez donc le plaisir peut-être de l'entendre encore – puisque vous êtes si harmonique qu'il me fait beaucoup de plaisir de vous voir ici.'*

Here was a compliment to be savoured, as well as an incentive to attend the next rehearsal. She went there with her stepmother the following week – it would have been unthinkable for a young unmarried girl to go to the theatre alone. Pacchierotti's part was 'divine indeed' and she was delighted when, at the beginning of the last act, he caught sight of them and came over smiling to their box. He looked very pale, thought Susanna, and had told her father earlier that he was far from well and that the rehearsal (owing to the lengthy dances woven into it) had almost killed him. There was time for only a brief exchange before he returned to the stage, Susanna complimenting him on his singing, Pacchierotti apologising for having failed to call on them that week, but it was enough to make Susanna's day. 'Lady Hales and Miss Coussmaker had wanted me all the Morng. to come and sit with them, but besides that I did not choose to leave my [step]mother, I wd. not have loſt Pacchierotti's bit of speech to me for the world.'

Susanna did not go to the first night of the opera but heard from her father that it had gone off very well, though poor Pacchierotti's scene in the last act, in which Rinaldo, surrounded by furies, cuts down the myrtle to break Armida's spell, had been ruined by a scuffle on the stage when some of the furies' torches went out. This had set the audience laughing, so that Pacchierotti could scarcely sing a note and had only recovered himself at the end. 'Had I been there,' wrote Susanna, 'I shd. have been ready to cry with disappointment & vexation, as nothing in the opera affeted me so greatly as the composition and performance of this scene.'

When Pacchierotti called two days later, he was able to describe the incident more fully. 'Oh! I was so angry Ma'am,' he told Mrs Burney. 'My beſt scene in the laſt act it was quite spoil'd…Four *disgraziate Furie! Ungrateful Furies*, they came out & by their bad action & ridiculous manners they made all the People laugh, & indeed I could not tell how to go on – & all the time they kept beating me like a Martyr – You see Ma'am my face how it is bruised.'

Susanna saw that a large discoloured mark on his face which she had mistaken for dirt was in fact a bruise, caused by a blow – only one of many which he had received on his head and shoulders, either deliberately or inadvertently while the Furies were milling around in the dark.

'I spoke to them in every language I knew and bid them ſtop,' he said, 'it is enough – *baſta* – *c'eſt assez* – indeed when I found they would not desiſt, I had a great will to ſtrike them myself, I felt such…such *rabbia* – Rage – Indeed – & then the

Newspaper the next day they put it in that I was embarrassed, & sung too much at private concerts. Now on a first night I never exert myself so much – I never felt more *impegno*…more desire to succeed – but these *dirty scrubs*…Indeed they quite made me mad.'

The whole episode, according to Curtis Price, sounded suspiciously like a hired cudgelling; the finger pointed at Tenducci, a former leading castrato, now a disgruntled hanger-on at the King's Theatre, who was consumed with jealousy of Pacchierotti. When Susanna went to a public performance of *Rinaldo* a few days later, the furies, who had been drilled in an extra rehearsal, stayed at a respectful distance from Pacchierotti. But there were 'some Beasts in the House, (Tenducci I *saw* & firmly believe to have been one of them),' wrote Susanna, 'who blew their noses, cough'd, spit and did everything possible but *hiss* during every one of his songs in a shameful manner – they meant to disturb him & make him sing ill and out of tune, to prevent people from hearing him & persuade everyone that the Public wish'd not to listen to him…Is it not enough to make one Sick that there shd. be such envy and such worthlessness in the World?'

She was happy to report that despite their efforts Pacchierotti sang angelically and was encored so strongly at certain points that the interruptions were inaudible. This was not at all to the taste of Piozzi, another jealous presence at the opera, who to Susanna's disgust had seated himself behind her in the pit, though she had done her best to avoid him on coming in.

'I could not have a more unwelcome neighbour,' she wrote, 'for though he *allowed* the *Music* of Rinaldo to be fine, I saw it wd. be dangerous to praise anything that was sung by Pacchierotti, & that he looked as black and blank as the deuce whenever he was on stage.' Piozzi never once applauded while

Pacchierotti was singing but, though he normally detested Madame Le Brun, insisted on encoring her violently. 'Mais est ce que vous dites encore pour vous moquer d'elle?' Susanna asked him laughing. 'Et pourquoi ne voulez vous pas que je dise encore Mademoiselle?' he said proudly. 'C'est trop juste – pourquoi ne faut il pas qu'elle répète son air *aussi?*' 'So because Pacchierotti sung like a Divinity & enchanted all that had ears, & were not devoured by Envy and Malice,' concluded Susanna, 'it was *trop juste* that Made Le Brun should likewise be encored.'

Almost entirely concentrated on the music, Susanna seldom mentioned the settings of the operas she attended, usually stock pieces from the theatre's store of scenery: a temple, a grove, a garden or triumphal arch. Sometimes there were special effects: shipwrecks and thunderstorms were favourite themes. In *Rinaldo,* however, the staging must have been unusually elaborate: she described it as being 'very good & *machinery* not bad – I like all but some *Monsters* who in the first scene are supposed to terrify Ubaldo from pursuing his way to Armida's enchanted Palace, but who appeared so very *tame*, that one longs to pat their heads & caress them like a good natured Pomeranian Dog.'

Susanna was having 'a prodigious gadding week'. Besides the visit to the opera there had been an evening with Lady Hales in Brook Street, 'which turned out delightfully in all respects but one, which was that it procured me scarce any conversation with Pacchierotti'. The room was crowded with company when she entered and, though Lady Hales immediately took her by the hand and seated her next to Lady Clarges, she felt so disconcerted by her entrance that it was some time before she had the *'dacity'* to look round. But Lady Clarges was all cordiality, insisting that she should come and see her, settling that she should call that Saturday if she could. 'But you never *try* anybody else's door,' said Miss Louisa Harris, who was sitting on the other side, invitingly. Susanna, unwilling to push herself forward – Miss Harris, a well known amateur singer, came from a much grander background than herself – merely laughed and looked down. 'I wish,' went on Miss Harris after a little pause, 'you would try somebody else's door.' But before she could pursue the subject further Lady Hales swept down on them and the moment was lost. 'I was half sorry,' wrote Susanna wistfully, 'because I shd. like to visit Miss L.Harris next beſt I think to Ly. Clarges of almoſt anybody I know if I had proper encouragement to do so.'

It seemed to be an evening of missed opportunities. Pacchierotti was surrounded by fashionable admirers, and she had no more than a few minutes' conversation with him. For much of the evening he was monopolised by Sir Thomas Clarges, Lady Clarges' husband, and later by Lady Clarges and Miss Harris. At the end of the evening, after Pacchierotti's final song had been applauded, Miss Harris commenced 'quite a flirtation with him at the bottom of the room'. Lady Clarges declared that she was so jealous that she would hiss her, which she did for quite a time, to the great amusement of Bertoni. Susanna would have liked to stay longer, but her father hurried her off, 'wch. I did not half like while Pacchierotti and the Harris's remained behind! – but I acknowledge myself insatiable on these occasions'.

Luckily there was soon another chance to see him, at a rehearsal of his next opera, Bertoni's *Il Finto Principe*, which she attended with her stepmother. They met Pacchierotti alighting from his carriage; he seemed delighted to see them but warned them that there would be a great many *da capos,* as it was only the first rehearsal. Susanna assured him that she was never tired on such occasions and, meeting him again on leaving, said all she could in praise of the music. 'I am very happy if you are content,' he told her, 'because in my opinion, I *value* it more highly than hardly anybody's.' He promised to come and see them that evening if he could get away in time, but to Susanna's regret did not appear.

The next morning Lady Hales came to take Susanna for a ride in the park. 'The day was heavenly…But you will pity me surely when I tell you that about half an hour after Ly Hales had carried me off, *Pacchierotti* called – not having been able to get away the night before from the party he was with. – It was so sweet in him to come – so good – so charming – and then that I should be out – Monſtrous i' fac!'

Susanna would have been more disappointed if she had not known he would be singing at a benefit concert for the great violinist Giardini at the Opera House next day. He came up to her smiling in the interval. 'Oh Miss Burney – how do you do? I am very happy to see you – I called upon you yeſterday, but I was so *unfortunate* not to find you at home!' She told him how vexed she had been at it. 'Oh,' said he, 'I hope to repay myself very soon.' They were then joined by Dr Burney, who told him how delighted he had been by his singing, though Pacchierotti confessed that he had been suffering greatly from stage fright. They both poured out their praises warmly. 'You spoil me when you sing, Signor Pacchierotti,' said Susanna, 'for everything else – before you begin I am occupied by thoughts of the pleasure I have to come, & after you sing everything is flat and insipid.' She hoped they would see him at their house the following week. 'Maybe…' he said. 'Indeed I am not master of my own time, or else I should tire you by coming very often but every day there are so many engagements for me!' 'Now ought I not to cry,' she wrote, 'that I missed seeing him when he called, now that I have only a paltry Maybe to live upon for next week.'

The second half of the evening went even better than

the first, with Pacchierotti's singing as the chief attraction. Susanna had never heard him sing so well before. 'His voice was so clear, so full, so sweet & free from every imperfection, he sung with such spirit, such feeling – such animation! – such freedom – such passion! Oh Dear, Oh Dear – how he did sing – I could scarce contain myself.'

When the last song was ended, she wrote, 'the applause was *universal* & was kept up for several minutes, indeed till he had quite left the Orchestra, which he did bowing, smiling & colouring, for he showed a great deal of Emotion in his Countenance, & felt in a degree the sensations he had excited in his hearers.'

After the performance, knowing his special interest in Pacchierotti, every one crowded round Dr Burney to congratulate him on his reception. Lady Mary Duncan looked in heaven; Sir Thomas Clarges came up to Susanna specially to say: 'There never was such a singer – Certainly there never was such a singer!' Piozzi spoke to her *en passant* but walked off when he saw Pacchierotti and Bertoni approach, 'which indeed I was not sorry for,' she wrote. Pacchierotti hardly stopped to speak to anybody, though every one tried to catch hold of him, but smiled and bowed to her before hurrying off with Bertoni. Lady Clarges came bustling up to her soon after: 'Good God! How Pacchierotti did sing! – Did you ever hear anything like him?' She was joined by Miss Harris and her friend, Mrs Brudenell, and a curious dispute arose between the two younger ladies. 'Do you know,' said Lady Clarges to Susanna, 'that she [meaning Miss Harris] is now quite *Notorious* with Pacchierotti – you know we observed her at tea with Lady Hales – she was then quite bad – but now there is really no supporting it – first with Rauzzini [another well known castrato] – then Pacchierotti – it's really being what I call quite common!'

'Miss L.H. answered her in the same style,' wrote Susanna, '& Mrs Brudenell sd. they were *both so much in love* with Pacchierotti & so jealous of him she did not know how to keep the peace between them – Ly Clarges told Miss L.H. she never intended to go anywhere with her again – that she was too bad! – &…so she ran on in a comical, wild manner, till I espied Pac: & Bertoni waiting at the bottom of the Room for his Carriage. "Lord sd. Lady C. let us all go & assail him – we can have him nicely up in that corner" – Miss L.H. urged her on, & Mrs Brudenell followed. I saw them very busy about him till his coach was called.'

Susanna would not have been sorry to join them but was buttonholed at that moment by a tall, boring clergyman, whom she had met with Lady Hales, and could not get away. Perhaps it was better so; there was an element of foolery, even prurience, about their attitude that was very different from her own more sensitive and serious approach.

On May 12 Fanny returned home for ten days while Mrs Thrale was seeing to affairs in Southwark, and Susanna's journal for the period almost ceased. But Pacchierotti, of course, came to call while she was there. He had just spent the morning with Sheridan, and this at least Susanna felt worth recording.

'He spoke with *delight* at having heard Mrs Sheridan sing, & the Linley family who were with her, & with such candour of Mr S as made me like him more than ever…He sd. that in Mr Sh's presence 'twas impossible not to feel the *ascendancy* he was capable of gaining over the minds of those he conversed with – that he had assured him that morning he wd. *in future* be more attentive to matters of business with Pacchierotti – "Pray do Sir, sd. I clasping my hands; for you have all that belongs to a Man of Genius, & of Honour – except *punctuality* – he laughed so!!" Wch. he might – I hope he feels it too

– however they parted excellent friends.'

On May 20 – just as Jem, on the far side of the world, was setting off from the Cape – Fanny went back to Bath again with Mrs Thrale. 'Oh my dear Fanny – it is very disagreable to have you only to lose you,' wrote Susanna next day. If Pacchierotti and Bertoni had not come to call that morning, she told her, she would hardly have had the spirit to pick up her pen. As it was she and Charlotte spent a happy half hour with them, Pacchierotti teasing her and himself for English and Italian words, while Bertoni leafed through a volume of Metastasio in search of inspiration. 'Oh! how agreable they are,' said Pacchierotti half aside on leaving them, 'Indeed – I don't know anybody so agreable as Dr Burney's family.'

Susanna concluded her journal for Fanny the following evening with an account of various other visitors and outings – 'I think I lead a moſt dissipated life.' It was the last letter she would write before London was engulfed in the fury of the Gordon riots, and for five terrifying days all normal life was overturned.

IX

On Friday June 2, 1780, a vast crowd of Londoners marched in procession to the Houses of Parliament. Sporting blue cockades and shouting anti-papist slogans, they were presenting a 'protestant petition' to Parliament against the supposed extension of Roman Catholic influence. Two years earlier a Roman Catholic Relief Bill, allowing a few minor concessions to Catholics while leaving them still largely excluded from public life, had passed through both Houses of Parliament without a division. It was an innocuous measure, chiefly designed to provide extra manpower by making it possible for Catholic recruits to join the army without foreswearing their religion. But it had aroused a storm of protest among extremist protestants in England and Scotland, whose spokesman, a crackpot young aristocrat called Lord George Gordon, was now leading the procession.

As evening fell, the crowd was joined by rougher elements more interested in plundering and burning than in joining the shouts of 'No Popery'. After vainly attempting to break down the doors of the House of Commons, where they were routed by a troop of Horse Guards, the rioters surged eastwards towards Lincolns Inn Fields where they burned down the chapel of the Sardinian embassy, then proceeded to the Bavarian Embassy, whose chapel suffered the same fate. For the moment it seemed that they were sated. On Saturday and most of Sunday there were no further disturbances, but on Sunday evening the rioting began again with far greater violence. This time Catholic property was targeted; a Catholic chapel at Moorfields was burned down and the houses of several Catholics nearby were looted. The magistrates, fearful of reprisals, were reluctant to intervene. Troops were called in, but since they were forbidden by law to fire till a magistrate had read the Riot Act, and the magistrates were usually nowhere to be found, the rioters soon learned to disregard them.

By Monday June 5th, the date with which Susanna's next letter begins, London was in a state of anarchy. A stone's throw from Leicester Fields, the Burneys' house was in the thick of some of the worst disturbances. Susanna, watching from the observatory, or gleaning the latest news from visitors, was able to give her sister a detailed description of the riots – a first hand account so immediate and exciting that it is worth quoting at length.

'Ah my dear Fanny!' she wrote, 'How frightened & how miserable you muſt have been had you known what has been passing in St Martin's Street & indeed in almoſt every ſtreet in London.'

That afternoon she had been sitting alone in the parlour, while her parents and Charlotte were out at a party nearby, when William, the manservant, came in with a face of alarm. He told her that there was terrible rioting in the streets and that the mob were breaking windows in Queen's Street nearby and threatening to set fire to some of the houses because they were inhabited by Roman Catholics.

'We were soon to have some of this horrid work before our own eyes,' she wrote, 'for very shortly after my father &c. returned home, & I was regretting having missed a delightful party…we heard violent shouts & huzzas from Leicester Fields & William who went to see what was the matter return'd to tell us the populace had broken into Sir Geo: Savile's house [Savile had sponsored the Catholic Relief Bill] & were then emptying it of its Furniture which having piled up in the midst of the Square, they forced Sir George's servant to bring them a candle to set fire to it – They would doubtless have set the House itself on fire had not the Horse & Foot guards prevented them – since this time the House has been full of soldiers, to prevent it from being pulled to the Ground, wch. the Rioters have since attempted to do – the windows & even window Frames are however almost demolished, & it cuts a terrible figure. I was terrified & shocked extremely at the rage and *licence éffrenée* of the Mob – & all the horrors wch. followed this Evening's work were anticipated by my fears wch. proved to be but too well grounded – In our observatory the flames from Savile House illuminated the whole Square – & my knees went *knicky knocky* like the Frenchman's in Harlequin's Invasion at the sight – about two in the morning all seemed quiet again & we went to bed.'

The next morning, despite the previous night's alarms, Susanna went to call on Lady Clarges. They discussed *Rinaldo;* Lady Clarges lent her several songs from the opera to copy, which were all the more valuable, wrote Susanna, since the music was not going to be published. Lady Clarges had seen

Sacchini, the composer, the night before and heard that, so far, the foreign performers in London were not worried; two of them, in fact, had been bold enough to go and watch the chapel in Moorfields burning and had been forced to join in the cries of 'No Popery'.

Susanna then went on to have dinner (a meal which took place at four o'clock) with Lady Hales, taking her leave between six and seven, since she was expecting Esther and some friends for tea. She was surprised to find that not only Leicester Fields but St Martin's Street itself were so crowded that the coachman could not get through and that there was a huge bonfire at the far end of the street. The coachman, astonished and terrified, set her down at the corner and accompanied her to her door, where she just managed to make her way through the crowd. Inside, she found her stepmother and Charlotte 'half out of their wits' with fear.

'They told me that about an hour before, many hundred People came running down our ſtreet, Huzzaing and shouting, with a Blue Flag – that this particular spite was againſt *Juſtice Hyde*, who had a House towards the bottom of our Street & had been aćtive in trying to quell the rioters – He was fortunately not in his House, for had he fallen into their Hands I believe he wd. have been torn to pieces – however they broke into his House & aćted the same part they had at Sir G. S.'s the preceding night, but did their work much more thoroughly. From our windows we saw them throw chairs, tables, clothes, in short everything the House contained, & as there was too much furniture for *one* fire they made several, at diſtances sufficiently great to admit one or 2 people passing between them – at one time I counted *six* of these fires wch. reached from the bottom of the ſtreet up to the crossing wch. separates Orange & Blue Cross Street – such a scene I never before beheld! – as it grew dusk, the wretches who were dissolved in smoak & cover'd with duſt at the bottom of the ſtreet, wth. the flames glaring upon them & the fires between us, seemed like so many *Infernals*, & their actions contributed to assiſt the ressemblance they bore, for more fury & rage than they shewed in demolishing everything they met with cannot be imagined.'

One thing that struck Susanna, and made her feel that the mob was being secretly directed by someone higher, was the fact that they brought a fire engine with them so that while they pulled Hyde's house to pieces, throwing everything they found onto the flames, they ordered the engine to play on the neighbouring houses so that they did not catch fire. This, apparently, had happened in every place the rioters had attacked. (She was right: there was certainly a degree of organisation in the early stages of the riots, probably among the disaffected shopkeepers and small tradesmen who formed the hard core of Lord George's supporters; later, as the wilder elements of the mob took over, the situation became completely out of hand.)

In the midst of these scenes, Susanna's friend Miss Kirwan and Esther arrived, both terrified to death and making their way through the crowd with great difficulty. Another friend who had been expected sent a note to say that, after several fruitless attempts to reach the house, she had just returned home more dead than alive. Miss Kirwan left before dark with a servant; Esther remained behind to await her husband.

Early in the evening about 30 footguards with an ensign at their head marched into the street but the mob, far from being disconcerted by their arrival, greeted them with huzzas, shouting and clapping them on the back. 'The ensign made some speech to them,' wrote Susanna, 'but as I suppose he dared not oppose so many hundred People as were here assembled after a very short discourse wth. them, he turn'd round and march'd out of the ſtreet as he came…This was more alarming than anything for if the Military power could not act, & it was not fear'd by the Populace, what chance did there seem to be of an end to the outrages they might be disposed to commit.'

Meanwhile the destruction of Hyde's house continued. When it was emptied of all its furniture, the rioters tore out the windows and window frames and began to pull up the floors and the panels and fling them onto the bonfires. The flames grew so fierce that the neighbours (who had all hung blue ribbons from their windows to prove their anti-popish sentiments) begged them to stop since, despite the fire engine, there was a serious danger of the whole street catching fire. 'Upon this the Ringleaders gave the word, & away they all ran paſt our windows to the bottom of Leiceſter Fields, with lighted firebrands in their hands like so many Furies – each carried something from the fires in our Street, & that nothing might escape they made in Leiceſter Fields one great bonfire of them – & they continued pulling down Pannels, Doors &c. till between two & 3 in the morning to keep up the bonfire and totally deſtroy the poor house.'

After a while St Martin's Street grew emptier, as the rioters rushed off to seek new targets. Susanna with her sister and brother-in-law was standing at the window when she saw a group of about ten people looking up and shouting 'No popery!' Since this was a cry they had heard repeatedly all evening, they took no notice until one of the men pointed at them and said to the others. *They are all three Papiſts!*' 'For God's sake,' cried Esther to her husband, 'call out *No Popery* or anything.' Her husband seized his hat and huzzaed from the window. 'It went againſt me to hear him,' noted Susanna, 'tho' it seem'd no joke to be marked out by such wretches as *Papiſts*.' Luckily the gesture seemed to satisfy the group, who moved off with cries of *'God bless your honour.'*

As the street began to empty, various friends dropped in, one of them carrying a blue cockade which had been his passport through the mob. Sir Joshua Reynolds came to call on his way to see Burke, another supporter of the Catholic Relief Bill, whose house had been threatened with the same fate as Savile's. Susanna's cousin Edward Burney arrived with the momentous news that the rioters had burst through the gates of Newgate Prison, releasing all the prisoners there and then setting the place on fire.

'On travelling up to the Observatory,' wrote Susanna, 'I saw such a scene as I will never forget, or think of but with horror – our own square was rendered as light as day by the Bonfire from Justice Hyde's house, wch. recd. fresh fuel every moment – & on the other side we saw the flames ascending from Newgate – a fire in Covent Garden wch. proved to be [the magistrate] *Sir John Fielding's* House – & another in Bloomsbury square, wch. was at [the Lord Chief Justice] *Lord Mansfield's* – I need not dwell on the consternation wth. wch. I beheld these sights – it was indeed unspeakable…Miss Young, who has slept here since Monday night, when the riot at Savile House had greatly terrified her & I sat up till near 4 in the morning when the Bonfire in Leicester Fields was extinguished & the Rioters had left our part of town & were fled to join the devastation that was going on at Ld. Mansfield's – Fielding's – and Newgate.'

The next morning, Wednesday, June 7th, began quietly. The mob had left St Martin's Street, and only the gutted shell of Hyde's house and the piles of smouldering embers at one end recalled the violence of the previous day. As the morning went on, friends and relatives began to call and exchange their stories. Esther came first, with the news that her part of town was now as dangerous as theirs had been and that a guard had been killed while Lord Mansfield's house was being attacked.

The soldiers had actually fired on the mob, killing seven people including a convict just escaped from Newgate who was to have been hanged that day. ('There is *poetical* justice,' Susanna commented.) However, far from dispersing the crowd, it had only incited them to further fury and, not content with a bonfire in which Mansfield's priceless pictures, library and manuscripts had been destroyed, they had set fire to the house itself. A Catholic school nearby and the houses of six or seven Catholic families had been looted and their contents burned, which 'made my heart ach [sic] to think of,' wrote Susanna, 'as they must have proved the bitter ruin of so many poor innocent people who, because they are Catholic, have no hope of redress nor [can] even venture to complain of the injuries they have received.'

After Esther had left, Miss Reynolds, Sir Joshua Reynolds' sister arrived, with news that Mr Drummond, whose house was just opposite her brother's in Leicester Fields, was expected to be attacked that night, because his wife and family were Catholics. Then came the Paynes, who had been breakfasting with friends in Spring Gardens; the mistress of the house had informed them with tears in her eyes that she must move all her furniture, as their house too was threatened to be burned because her husband was a Justice of the Peace. More friends followed, each with their stock of rumours and alarms – then 'last but not least in love', Pacchierotti.

'I was astonished to see him,' wrote Susanna, '& to hear he came on foot – his Countenance was as serene as ever I saw it, & he declared to me he was not the least frightened – I dared not tell him how frightened I was myself for him – but indeed I was cruelly alarmed tho' I assured him, wch. at that time was very true, that for *myself* & those wth. whom I was intimately connected I had no fear, nor an idea of having any cause for fear – For others indeed I told him I could not help being under some anxiety, & I beg'd he wd. not expose himself by walking about alone at such a time as this – when the city seemed to be inhabited by Wild Beasts, not human Creatures – "Why should I fear," sd. he smiling, "I have committed no fault – but if it please God that I should meet any chastisement, it will be my duty to submit."'

'Oh God forbid! – God forbid!' cried Susanna, adding that she only meant that she begged him to be careful for the present. But Pacchierotti made light of her fears, though he told her that Bertoni had been terribly frightened at the sight of the flames from Sir George Savile's house two nights before and was still too afraid to come and visit them that morning. They talked for some time, Pacchierotti calm and good humoured, Susanna so distraught that she could scarcely remember what was said. One detail struck her forcibly: although most of their Italian and other Catholic acquaintances had removed their names from their front doors (Giardini even daubing 'No Popery!' on his), Pacchierotti had resisted all advice to do the same. Nor did he intend to put off a concert with a friend of the Burneys', Mrs Castle, which was due to take place that night, announcing that for his part one evening was as good as any other. 'What a Hero!' wrote Susanna, though on her father's advice the concert was afterwards postponed.

Soon after Pacchierotti left, her father came in 'harrassed to death' and completely unable to settle to any of his usual occupations. He went out shortly afterwards, first to urge Mrs Castle to put off her concert, then to warn Mr Drummond (whose daughter was one of his pupils) of the rumours that his house was due to be burned that evening. He came back again to face a new and more alarming situation: the morning's quiet, it seemed, was only the calm before a further storm.

X

Backing on to Dr Burney's premises in St Martin Street were a number of small shops in Long's Court, which he rented to various tradesmen. One of them, a Mr Porter, kept a china shop there. Soon after Dr Burney had gone out that morning, Porter came round asking to speak to him and was shown into the parlour where Susanna and her stepmother were sitting.

'He told us,' wrote Susanna, 'with a face of patient Misery wch. ſtruck me with the utmoſt commiseration that reports were spread about that *his* house was to be attacked that Night. – "Good God' – cried I – "Yours? – & for which purpose?" "Because ma'am…They say *we are Papiſts*" – "God bless my soul – but is it so?" At the time I ask'd the queſtion I had indeed no idea that it was or I shd. not have put it so abruptly, but by the poor man's countenance I was but too well convinced – "I was *educated Ma'am in those principles*" sd. he looking down. – "Oh for Heaven's sake sd. I interrupting the poor man, do not apologise for them to *us* – we are the laſt people who would wish you to be persecuted."'

They asked him what reasons he had for fearing that a house so small and private as his should be attacked. He told them that someone had heard one of the rioters outside Sir George Savile's house saying that there were two Papists' houses in Long's Court, mentioning his name and Riley's, a pawnbroker opposite, and that they would both be destroyed that night.

Susanna asked if Riley was a Roman Catholic. 'No

Ma'am,' he said, 'he is nothing at all – he is only a bad man.'
He then said that he had some very valuable china in his house
which he would use to compensate her father for the loss of his
rent and that he would bring it round immediately, adding that
he could bear his calamity patiently if he could give everyone
what he owed. 'I declare the poor Man's honesty brought tears
to my eyes,' wrote Susanna, 'and the Compassion I felt for his
case was such as you will readily conceive.' She immediately
tried to persuade him to pack up his most valuable things for
his own sake, not theirs, and to go to friends until the storm
was over, but he said he knew no-one that was not in the same
state as himself. Mrs Burney told him that she would ask him
to call again as soon as Dr Burney had returned, and the poor
man went away, leaving Susanna more alarmed than she had
ever been before.

Her father came in soon after, 'wth. no light heart I cd.
read in his countenance'. Mrs Burney told him that Porter had
been with them and that she wished he would persuade him to
leave his house. 'But my dear,' said Dr Burney before she could
explain the reason, '*I want to be gone Myself* – for I was told by
a person just now whose face even I don't know that the chapel
on the side of the house is down to be on fire to tonight.' (The
chapel in fact was a Huguenot church, where the services were
held in French – for the rioters the fact that they were in a foreign language was crime enough.)

'I now found,' wrote Susanna, 'that we were likely to be
in the most imminent danger ourselves – that our House wd.
be burnt & pillaged in all probability, & that inevitable ruin
must follow my beloved Father & all that belong to him – the
Chapel on one side of our House – Porter's House at the back
of it – the Pawnbroker's on the other side – Mr Drummond's
in Leicester Fields, & the House nearly opposite us, the corner
of Blue Cross Street, – that for having recd. some of Mr Justice

Hyde's things, & secreted his men from the fury of the Rioters, were all destined that horrid night to the Flames. – There was not the slightest reason to hope that *our* House encircled by so many fires shd. escape being consumed.'

The afternoon was spent in feverish planning. Dr Burney sent for Porter to talk things over. He first suggested that Porter should send his valuables to their house for safety, then realised that it was impossible to do so unobserved and that they would only be attacked themselves for doing so. Speaking to Porter 'with the goodness of an angel', he told him not to think of his landlord but to take away whatever was most valuable if he and his wife decided to leave their house. After Porter had gone, it was time to think of themselves. Mrs Burney, looking quite jaundiced with terror, was all for leaving for Samuel Crisp's at Chesington immediately. This however seemed a very wild scheme, since if their house escaped the flames it would certainly be pillaged by the rioters, and if it were to be set fire to with no-one in it there would be no chance of saving anything. Dr Burney was in such a state of consternation that he did not seem to know what course to take – the Drummond family, he learned, had already left their house in Leicester Fields, but Mr Drummond was staying behind himself to wait upon events.

In the end Susanna suggested that they should pack up some of their things and send them to Esther Burney, or their friends the Boyles and the Kirwans, whose houses were in less vulnerable areas. They accordingly packed up their plate, and Dr Burney took it in their coach to the Boyles. When he returned he found Barry, the painter, and Miss Reynolds taking tea in the parlour, but soon after Miss Reynolds's servant came in with the news that the house of Mr Cove, a distiller in Great Queen Street, was on fire and that many others were alight, and she had not the courage to stay any longer. Baretti came in a little later, assuring them that there were so many soldiers in the neighbourhood that they were not in the least danger – 'however, as we had seen the way in which the Guards had behaved when Mr Justice Hyde's house was attacked,' wrote Susanna, 'this gave us little consolation.'

As soon as Baretti had gone, she helped her father pack up his most precious manuscripts in large paper bags, which were sent with William in the coach to Esther's house in Tavistock Street. They then sent off a second coachful with her parents' clothes and various other portables – 'I leave you to imagine the feelings we had during these preparations,' she wrote. William soon came back however, with the news that Tavistock Street was now so full of rioters that he had not felt it safe to carry them there. It was now too late to send them to the Kirwans, and they could do no more, but the added fear of what might be happening to Esther and her family was almost unbearable, especially as William told them that there were several raging fires nearby.

That night, the night of June 7-8, saw the worst conflagrations of all. The skies above London were lit up like an inferno. The King's Bench, the Marshalsea and Fleet prisons were set on fire. A huge distillery in Holborn, with half a dozen houses close to it, exploded into flames – Vesuvius, said the twelve-year-old Dick, was nothing to it. The gutters ran with blazing spirits, and many rioters were burned to death as they lay intoxicated in the smouldering ruins. Susanna and her family stood watching from the observatory, expecting at any moment that the chapel and Porter's house would be attacked and listening to the distant sounds of shouts and screams and shots without knowing where they were coming from. At two in the morning, things seemed quieter, and Susanna persuaded her father to lie down, though as on the previous night he refused to undress or go to bed. She herself stayed up with Miss Young for another two hours; then having taken a last look from the observatory, where the smoke from the distillery was rising as high as the flames had done before, they crept into bed.

The next morning, Thursday June 8, there was no sign of further trouble in their neighbourhood, though fires were still breaking out elsewhere and a number of the rioters, having demolished the London houses of Fielding and Hyde, were surging towards their country houses with the intention of destroying them as well. Dr Burney rose early and set out on foot to see the damage in the city, passing the ruins of Newgate, where people were wandering as freely as in the piazzas of Covent Garden, and those of the distillery in Holborn Place, still littered with bodies of the drunk or dead. He visited the Bank of England, where the troops defending it had fired on a crowd the previous night, killing seventeen people and successfully repelling three attempts to storm it. Here he was able to draw out some money, being determined, he said, that even if he was ruined he would at least have the satisfaction of having paid off all his debts.

He returned home for a hasty breakfast, then hurried off again, 'all activity, all animation', visiting Esther and his sisters, calling on creditors and friends and remonstrating with those he knew in government on the weakness of the magistrates and the need to take firm measures against the mob. In this, as he learned, he was preaching to the converted. At a special meeting of the Privy Council the night before, the King had taken the lead in questioning the law which made it impossible for troops to act without a magistrate's permission: the troops, it was agreed, should now be ordered to suppress the rioting whatever the magistrates might do. It was some time however before the orders could be put into practice, and for much of the day the outbursts of violence continued. There were still rumours that the houses in Long's Court, and Mr

Drummond's in Leicester Fields, were to be set on fire, and Susanna spent the afternoon packing up books and papers to be sent to safety. She was beginning to make a parcel of her own clothes when, shortly after six o'clock, her father returned with the news that the troops were now in control of the city; military camps had been set up in St James's Park and Hyde Park, and most of the rioters had been arrested or dispersed. The mood of the household changed in a moment from gloom to exultation, '& since that time,' wrote Susanna, 'I have done nothing but thank God every moment for the escape we have had, & the yet greater escape which the poor Catholic inhabitants of this place have had from the rage of a set of savages'.

Her father's first thought, after telling his own family, was to go and give the good news to the Porters, whom he left pouring blessings on his head. 'I declare I was myself so affected for the poor man that I almost cried with joy when my Father told me how happy he had been making him,' wrote Susanna. At nine in the evening William brought word that Lord George Gordon had been arrested and taken to the Tower, without the slightest opposition from the populace. For the first time since Monday evening, they were able to go to bed with a quiet mind.

While London had been at the mercy of the mob, Fanny had been almost beside herself with worry for her family. 'My dearest Sir,' she wrote to her father, 'How are you? where are you? and what is to come next? The accounts from town are so frightful, that I am uneasy, not only for the city at large, but for every individual I know in it. I hope to Heaven that ere you receive this, all will be once more quiet; but till we hear that it is so, I cannot be a moment in peace.'

In Bath, the first intimation of trouble had been the arrival of the stage coaches from London, all chalked with the words 'No Popery.' Newspaper accounts gave some impression of the rioting, but Fanny still had no idea of the danger her family was in. On Friday, June 8, a Catholic chapel in Bath and the house of the priest belonging to it was burned down. 'We saw the flames & heard the shouts together one whole dreadful night,' wrote Mrs Thrale. Saturday morning, to Fanny's inexpressible concern, brought no news from her family, but Mrs Thrale had letters from a friend, Sir Philip Clerke, and Perkins, her brewery manager, to say that her town house and the brewery had been attacked three times and that the house at Streatham was also under threat. On the same day, a paragraph in one of the Bath and Bristol papers asserted that Mr Thrale (who had voted for the Catholic Relief Bill) was a papist. 'This villainous falsehood,' wrote Fanny, 'terrified us even for his personal safety, and Mrs Thrale and I agreed that it was best to leave Bath directly and travel about the country.'

The family set out in a coach and four, taking a circuitous route from village to village (they preferred to avoid large towns) to Brighton. By Sunday Fanny's worst fears had been assuaged by the news that the rioting in London was over, but it was not until she reached Brighton on June 18, where letters from her family awaited her, that she received a full account of what had happened. The Thrales too had had a narrow escape. The brewery in Southwark had been invaded by a mob, and it was only through the courage and quick wits of the manager Perkins, who had offered them free beer and food, that they had been saved from ruin.

Fanny was now desperate to get home; her lengthy absences had made her feel an alien from her family, and their recent perils made her long to see them more than ever. In London, the disturbances had died down, though the memory of the destructive fury of the mob would remain in the background of men's minds, to be revived only nine years later by the news of the storming of the Bastille. No-one who had experienced the Gordon Riots, with its images of flames and terror, would be likely to underestimate the dangers of the French Revolution.

Susanna, whose first action after calm was restored was to write a 'full and minute' account of the riots to her sister, was soon returning to her usual interests, the opera and, inevitably, Pacchierotti. Her father had heard him at the opera on Saturday, finding the theatre very ill attended and most of the Italian singers in a state of terror, though Pacchierotti, 'as superior in courage as in talents', gave one of his best performances. He called at St Martin's Street with Bertoni the following day. Susanna congratulated him on his bravery during the riots.

'Indeed,' said he, 'I know it is very *foolish* – perhaps I exposed myself a little by it – but ever since I was a little boy, if I heard there was any dispute – any quarrel, I always ran to see what was the matter – I have sometimes put myself in great danger by it – but I cannot help it – it is *Instinct* I believe. Once I heard a great noise, a great quarrel, when I was walking late at night – in Italy – & I ran as fast as I could – when I came to the place I saw several men fighting with knives – and a priest who knew me said – *Pacchierotti come away – you are very ill advised to stay there, for you don't know how many innocent people they may be killed* and indeed it was very dangerous – it was so dark and those men they strike about with their knives without any fear.'

He told her that Mrs Castle had written to him the previous Wednesday telling him that she was postponing her concert party *'as he must be afraid of going out during such terrible times'*. 'But indeed,' he said laughing, but a little affronted, 'I believe she was more afraid than me – I think she should have mentioned a little her own fears as well as mine.' In fact he had deliberately gone walking through Spring Gardens, where she lived, and many other parts of the city while the riots were at their height. 'How could he *hasarde* himself so!' wrote Susanna.

It was now drawing near the end of the opera season, when Pacchierotti and Bertoni were to leave London, with no engagement yet arranged for the next year. Neither he nor Bertoni had received their arrears of salary from Sheridan. At the opera house the previous night, Sheridan had gone up to Pacchierotti of his own accord (having previously missed appointments twice before) and arranged to meet him at the Treasurer's office after the performance. Needless to say, there was no sign of Sheridan when the time came, and Pacchierotti had decided to send him a note threatening legal proceedings, which he showed to Susanna to correct. As far as she could remember it ran as follows:

'Pacchierotti presents his respectful Comp's to Mr Sh. & has waited till this time in hopes of hearing something from him. He wished much to spare Mr Sheridan from the disturbance of the Law, for the sake of the sincere Esteem he has for him – he thinks his conduct towards Mr Sheridan during this engagement is without the least reproach – nevertheless he must be obliged to act differently as he is under present neccessity for Money which gives him great concern for the reason above mentioned.

'He hopes Mr Sheridan will likewise remember his Friend Mr Bertoni.'

Pacchierotti stayed talking with Susanna and Mrs Burney some time longer, Pacchierotti arguing playfully about points of English grammar – 'he would not use say *to* me instead of *say me*,' wrote Susanna – and full of enquiries about Fanny. He complained that Mrs Thrale had kept her away from London far too long. Susanna stoutly sang her praises. 'Indeed Ma'am! I am very glad of it,' said Pacchierotti, 'because she deserve to have such a Friend as Miss Fanny.' 'And you Miss Susan,' he added, *'Indeed!'* Susanna was touched. 'You know he has not the heart to speak in praise of anybody before my face without including me,' she wrote. Meanwhile Bertoni, who could not follow the conversation, looked over some new music by Sacchini which was lying on the harpsichord and at last, after trying several pieces, insisted on dragging his friend away. Pacchierotti, thought Susanna, seemed in no hurry to leave; for him perhaps, as well as for her, his approaching departure made every conversation doubly precious. It was small consolation to Susanna when Barry and Baretti arrived to spend the rest of the evening – 'the latter smothering me with his love,' she wrote. With her thoughts still full of Pacchierotti, she had no time for either gentleman.

XI

There was a further instalment of the Sheridan saga to relate when Pacchierotti next called at St Martin's Street.

'Friday night [June 16] – I was interrupted this Morng in writing to you by no unwelcome visitors – Pacchierotti & Bertoni,' wrote Susanna to her sister. 'I ran downstairs instantly...my Mother followed me into the Room – & after asking her how she did, he sd. – "Indeed ma'am you look so well that it is not useful to make the enquire"...Bertoni hoped I had got over a troublesome cold I had when they were here Sunday.

'"Indeed" sd. Pacchierotti, "she look better Miss Susan – I am not well – but *I* should be better if Mr Sheridan he would pay me."'

Susanna asked him whether anything was yet settled with Sheridan. He had sent his note, he told her; Sheridan had not answered – he almost never answered letters – but had come round to see him instead. *'Mr Pacchierotti,'* he said, *'What a shocking letter you have sent me!'* 'Indeed Sir,' said Pacchierotti, 'I am at a loss to do it myself but my neccessity for money it urge me to take such a step.' Sheridan then told him that he had been disappointed in some money he was expecting – perhaps because of the Gordon riots – but would certainly pay him very soon. 'But, Sir,' said Pacchierotti, 'I *cannot wait* no longer...my friend Mr Bertoni he has nothing more to do here, and he escaped a very good opportunity to travel in Italy only because he could not get his money – indeed it is very disagreable.' It was very true, said Sheridan soothingly, but Bertoni could make his arrangements to leave England the following

Monday, since he would definitely be paid before that time.

'This passed last Monday,' concluded Pacchierotti, '& tomorrow it is Saturday, & we have heard nothing more from Mr Sheridan – I believe he *lies* as usual...but tomorrow night when the curtain drops, if Mr Sheridan he does not send to me or speak with me before, I shall, indeed, become very *clamourous*.'"

Susanna exclaimed at Sheridan's behaviour, remarking that it was quite a new thing for performers at the King's Theatre to have such trouble in getting paid.

'He is indeed,' said Pacchierotti, 'the moſt neglectful man in the world – of his own intereſt – I am at a loss to take measures againſt him because I believe he has a good heart – and he is a man of such a pleasing demeanour – so gentle – *tanto amore*, that whenever I see him I always have the hope that he is going to change, and that he will not play me any more tricks.'

Like so many performers before and after him who suffered at his hands, Pacchierotti found it impossible to be angry with Sheridan. As one of his later victims once remarked, if only some enchanter had given him possession of a fortune he would immediately have been transformed into a being of the nicest honour and most unimpeachable moral excellence. Unfortunately the enchanter never materialised.

On this occasion some kind of solution was found when Sheridan, after further shuffling and excuses, persuaded the performers to extend the season beyond June 30, when Pacchierotti's contract ended. The additional performance took place on July 1st, thus enabling Pacchierotti to earn Sheridan the money he already owed him. Whether, even then, he was paid in full remains uncertain, for Susanna's letter-journals, the only source of information on the matter, end with her sister's return from Bath ten days before.

In the meantime there was much to tell her and a round of farewell visits and performances for Pacchierotti. 'I asked him,' wrote Susanna, 'if he could come & take leave of Ly. Hales in the evng. as I shd. be there & she wd. leave London on Sunday – but he could not being engaged the whole day – "very well" sd. I – "We shall come & see *you* tomorrow – at the Opera House"…He was afraid he sd. he shd. keep me from paying my visit – but said he wd. come in the Evng next week – & Morning too – I wish he may keep his word – "but" sd. he, "I ought not to come too often because it makes it harder for me to leave you – Indeed I know it" – I felt 'twould be the same thing wth. me – & half said so – *"Never mind it"* sd. poor Pacchierotti smiling – but his eyes really glistened.'

The loneliness of Pacchierotti's position, the essential deprivation to which he owed his dazzling triumphs as a singer, would always sound a note of tragedy to those who knew him well. With the moment of his departure drawing near, the poignancy of his situation struck Susanna afresh. Nor was her own heart immune. Those long delightful conversations at St Martin's Street, the evenings when his voice transported his hearers, meant still more now they were coming to an end. She longed to see Fanny and discuss her feelings. 'I begin to grow sick & I dare not tell you why,' she wrote, '…Oh that you could have returned to us in London instead of making such an endless tour.'

But her mood had changed by the time she took up her pen again late that evening: 'Pray burn this Journal or put it away unread unless you can with fortitude hear the enjoyments you have missed – I am in a hundred minds whether to journalise to you or not! – but you desire me to write & be minute – so if you can't bear it now…don't read my letter.'

Between six and seven, just after she had posted her letter to her sister, Lady Hales arrived by appointment with her two daughters, Marianne and Jane, and two young friends, Miss Coats and the seventeen-year-old Miss Sukey Ogle, an ardent devotee of Pacchierotti's. After tea they set off in two coaches, Lady Hales's and her father's, to the opera house. The house was filling up fast, but they found places in the second row of the gallery.

'I had the good fortune to be next to my dear Father,' wrote Susanna. 'Miss Coats was near me & very sincerely delighted & Miss Ogle is *dying* for Pacchierotti – but for her hopes of hearing him again at Mrs Caſtle's Monday or Tuesday, she told me I shd. have seen her faint away when the curtain dropt. She leaves London Wednesday next. Ly. Hales & Marianne were I believe the leaſt happy of the party as they wanted to be downſtairs *with the Ton.*'

Knowing the opera, *Rinaldo*, as well as she did, seemed to add to, rather than subtract from, the pleasure Susanna felt in listening to it. Her father too found it improved every time he heard it. On this particular occasion, perhaps because it was its last performance, the audience seemed exceptionally quiet and attentive, and apart from Madame Le Brun, who seemed to have a cold, the other performers sang unusually well.

'As to Pacchierotti,' wrote Susanna, 'I really believe he had never before sung so well in either of the nights I had before heard it performed…His firſt fine song he sang moſt perfeċtly in all respeċts, & with a dignity & grace in the slow part that was heavenly, & a freedom & spirit in the Allegro that was animating – in this & his other song he made the fineſt cadences in the world – & my Father who has such opportunities of watching him, says he never makes the same a second time – But he is *such* a singer – that really if I ever have the misfortune to meet people who do not feel his merit I shall despise them too much to think it worth while to attempt answering them – His Cantabile he sung in a grand, majeſtic, *simple* ſtyle the firſt time – he was encored in it in a more hearty & violent manner than I have ever heard him I think, for all the House seemed to unite their voices – & not *one* attempt was made to oppose the encore…The trio too wch. ends this aƈt was only wanting a hair of being repeated – In this scene & air with the Furies he almoſt dissolved us away – Oh Lord! how he did sing.'

The house was packed with Pacchierotti's admirers.

'Lady Clarges was in the ſtage box…& with her Mrs Brudenell & Ly Edgecumbe – all of them I doubt not in *extase* – Lady Mary Duncan was in the Pitt – Sir Thomas Clarges, Mr Brudenell, Mr Parsons, Rauzzini, the Miss Clarges & c &c. We came away before the laſt dance began, on the ſtairs Mr North met me, & beg'd that I wd. pity him as he was going out of town & shd. hear Rinaldo no more – nor Pacchierotti.'

London was beginning to empty for the summer, as its fashionable occupants moved off to their country estates. When Pacchierotti called at St Martin's Street the following night, June 18, he showed Susanna a note from the Burneys' friend Mrs Castle, asking him to fix a date for her cancelled concert. She suggested the next day, Monday, or Tuesday; Pacchierotti however could only offer Monday or Thursday, being engaged on the days in between. Susanna told him she hoped he would choose Monday, as a certain young lady (Sukey Ogle), who was leaving London before Thursday, had told her that she would die if she did not have the opportunity of hearing him again at Mrs Castle's. *'Indeed,'* said Pacchierotti, with a mixture of pleasure and surprise. Susanna exclaimed how well he had sung the previous night.

'Indeed,' he said again, with less surprise but still more satisfaction, *'you think it so Miss Susan?'*

'Oh, I am sure this time you muſt have thought it so yourself.'

'Indeed – as I knew you was to be there – I tried to make the evening as little tiresome to you as I could.'

'Oh Mr Pacchierotti,' cried Susanna, 'that is such a compliment…Indeed,' she went on, laughing, 'I believe you did not think of who was there – but you were finely in voice.'

'Very true – my voice was better I believe than usual – but do me justice Miss Susan… and believe what I tell you – I thought *so* much of your having told me you should be at the opera, that, as you did not tell me the place where you should sit, I looked *everywhere* – pit, boxes – gallery –'

'Oh – I am almost always in the gallery –'

'Indeed? – and as I am not very long sighted I could not distinguish you.'

'I told him we were a large party,' wrote Susanna, 'but not in the front row – but what a pretty compliment – how touching a one was this – well nobody knows how much they were obliged to *me* for his singing like a Divinity.'

Susanna's pleasure at this tribute was mixed with sadness. 'He is very good now,' she told Fanny, 'but for how short a time can I benefit from his being so! – 'tis this that made me sick when I wrote to you last night & which *mi turba l'anima* at this present moment.'

It was the nearest she would ever come to admitting her feelings for Pacchierotti, but the rest of her conversation with him that evening was closer and more revealing than any she had had before.

Pacchierotti talked to her of his experiences in London. Although his health had held up, except for his illness in the spring, he felt that his singing there had never really taken off. The warmth and enthusiasm of Italian audiences, to whom opera was their native element, had sustained and inspired him in his own country. In England, he had never felt the same rapport with his listeners.

'I should have sung better if I could ever have overcome my fear since I have been here – but never have I been able to do it…In other places where I have sung, I have always been diffident and frightened at first – for six or seven nights – but by degrees, when I found the public seemed pleased I grow – not *impertinent* with the public – but easy – familiar – then I feel such fondness for my profession, indeed, that my little genius, *which was a dwarf*, it becomes –' 'Gigantic,' prompted Susanna. '*Si, gigantesca* – but here indeed it never arrive to me – I am always so depressed – I cannot bear it – indeed, sometime, I feel myself so hurt at the noise and inattention and neglect of the people that I could die upon the stage.'

'But no performer since I remember has had such admirers as you,' said Susanna.

'Oh Miss Susan! – indeed I believe there are not twenty people who regard me as you do.'

'As *I* do? – Nay…but you are infinitely more generally admired for your talents Signor Pacchierotti, than you imagine – I am *sure* of it – In *our* family indeed you have a double claim to our regard – from *friendship* to yourself and sensibility of your talents.'

'Oh! Miss Susan – *Come e buona,*' said Pacchierotti turning to Bertoni who was listening, and in order not to exclude him from the conversation, Susanna carried on in French. 'But I'm sure,' she said in that language, 'that even if I didn't have the pleasure of knowing you personally, I'd be *crazy* about you when I heard you.'

'Oh! You're the most obliging creature in the world.'

'Me – not at all – but there are many people who feel the same – more than you can imagine – I don't so much say the people of high rank, because you know how many friends you have among them – but there are a number of people between the highest and the lowest ranks who hardly see you except at the opera, and who in consequence don't know you, who are full of enthusiasm for your talents.'

'Really – I've never been able to be convinced about that. As for those of high rank, I'm less at ease with them than you might think – I've never enjoyed the pleasure of genuine conversation or friendship with them – the moment I see them they want me to sing – and singing all the time is enough to make one die of boredom.'

Susanna knew it well. Although writers, actors and musicians were often invited to the houses of the aristocracy, they were regarded less as equals than as entertainers. Even Pacchierotti, for all the adulation he received, was to some extent a victim of this attitude. (It was for this reason that Sheridan, when he married, had refused to allow his wife to continue her career as a singer.) Knowing how pestered he was elsewhere, Susanna had always resisted asking Pacchierotti to sing – 'so much so,' she told him, 'that when you are with us I don't even want to mention music.'

'I mean *all the time*,' said Pachierotti, 'sometimes I like to sing for my own pleasure. But yours is the only house where I'm allowed to be like other people – and as you can imagine one needs about five or six of those to be happy in a town like this. But I'm obliged to live alone – or fall in with the Italian riff-raff here, and listen to enough gossip in a quarter of an hour to make me ill for two days – I hate my countrymen when they're in this country – or go to English houses and be snubbed by the words "Not at home".'

'But no-one would say that to you!'

'It happens to me – as it does to other people – but I expose myself to it as little as possible.'

'I can't believe that – I know so many people who envy us for having the pleasure of your company, who are always saying, *"Oh if only Pacchierotti would come to us, as he does to you."*

'Ah! But they say that to me too – but they add – *if you would let me know.* Ah! that *let me know* is enough to kill me.'

'*Mon Dieu*, Signor Pacchierotti – and I've said it to you so often, without ever imagining…'

'No, but listen,' said Pacchierotti, interrupting, 'at your house one can come and go as one likes – there's so little ceremony that that *let me know* is quite unnecessary – but when anyone else says it, I always think I'm not wanted unless I've been invited.'

'Who could have imagined he cd. have put such a construction as this,' wrote Susanna, though he went on to assure her that he'd never heard the words 'not at home' in St Martin's Street.

'Oh, never for you, I'm certain,' she told him.

'But for others?'

'Very rarely – sometimes if I've got letters to write, or something to do, I tell the servants to say I'm not at home – but whenever *you* arrive they know how mortified I'd be if you heard those words and they'd never let you go away.'

'But I'm afraid I may have bothered you at times.'

'No, *never.*'

'But when that is the case, why don't you say "Pacchierotti, I'm busy now – I have something to do for an hour – two hours – any time – *but call again.*"'

'Ah,' said Susanna, reverting briefly into English, 'I will tell you if ever my inclination prompts me to do anything but converse with you when you call here – but since you say there are so few houses where you have visited on terms so friendly and familiar as ours, I think we ought to have benefitted more from it by seeing you oftener.'

'I feared always to be too importunate.'

'Oh – you jest.'

'No truthfully – I'm speaking seriously and sincerely – I've seen that the English nation is very difficult to get to know – they're – shy – reserved – they find foreigners, poor devils that they are, a nuisance – all the same, I've been shown great courtesy and many examples of friendship and kindness since I've been here.'

'But Signor Pacchierotti…'

'But listen to me,' he said, interrupting, *You are English* – and I've always thought in consequence that you'd be bored if you saw me too often – Dr Burney is very busy – Madame also sometimes has visits or something else to do – it could be the same thing with you.'

'Ah, *Mon Dieu*, it's not possible – it's an excuse!' cried Susanna.

'No, no, it is not an excuse,' he said in a tone so serious and decided that Susanna was astonished and concerned, 'You must know that, quite apart from music, the special sympathy that I have for you, for your conversation, makes your company far too valuable for me not to wish to come more often. If I hadn't been afraid that despite all your kindness I'd have become a burden to you…'

'Ah *Mon Dieu!* – I never could have conceived that you should seriously think such things – but at present, you no longer think so?'

'No, it is true.'

'Oh, why did you ever think so – you've said it to make me ill for two days, I think, because from now on I"ll always be thinking how many more times you might have come here. But now,' she said, switching back to English again, 'I must, I must talk English to you.'

'Indeed,' said he smiling, 'It will be more useful to me – we have made a long conversation in French.'

'Now that you no longer have such suspicions of us, Signor Pacchierotti – you will come oftener.'

'Oh! but I shall have so little time to spend here – [in] two weeks you will be rid of the trouble of me.'

'Was this not a heart breaking speech?' wrote Susanna. That Pacchierotti, whose visits she so looked forward to and treasured, could have felt so uncertain of his welcome, was something she could not have imagined. 'How could he doubt our wishing to see him oftener – I cannot conceive and am much disturbed and chagrined.'

Pacchierotti and Bertoni stayed a little longer, arranging that if Mrs Castle's concert was to be the following day he would spend a whole evening with them on Thursday. 'And if she fixes on Thursday, tomorrow?' asked Susanna. 'I don't know, indeed,' he said, laughing, '…but Thursday there will have passed some intermediate days – some time of rest for you.'

Susanna would not let him continue, begging him not to pain her by doubting the pleasure they had in his company. At last he said, with a joking reference to the phrase he hated, that he 'would let her know' and promised to send her a note the next day. Soon afterwards he took his leave. 'Sweet creature,' sighed Susanna mournfully. She had not even had the courage to ask if he would be coming back to London the following season, though the question had been on the tip of her tongue all evening. She was afraid that his troubles with Sheridan would have put such ideas out of his head. If so, their parting would be sadder still.

XII

Early on Monday morning, June 19, the Burneys had word from Mrs Castle that her concert party would take place that evening. At one o'clock however, Susanna received a note from Pacchierotti, its English somewhat incoherent but its meaning clear enough.

'Mr Pacchierotti's compliments wait on Miss Burney. It is quite twelve in the morning & Mrs Castle has no message sent him yet for the evening, so that he does not know whether she intends to have him & his Friend [Bertoni] or not – he is only displeased on the uncertainty because he cannot fix other party to spend the evening as he would have done to comply his wishes with that of his friends in St Martin's Lane.'

Susanna was upstairs when Pacchierotti's note arrived, and was told that his servant had left without waiting for a reply. 'I was very sorry I cd. not answer it to tell him we were engaged to meet him that night at Mrs Castle's,' she wrote; 'I was amazed indeed that she shd. have delayed so late in sending him an answer.'

She thought no more about it, however, until she and her father arrived, rather late she feared, at Mrs Castle's. As it proved, they were early enough, for they were met at the head of the stairs by an agonised Miss Ogle, who told Dr Burney that 'a most shocking mistake had happen'd through her blundering in the world.' On the previous evening Mrs Castle had sent her Pacchierotti's note giving her the choice of Monday or Thursday, at the same time telling her that though Thursday would be more convenient for her, she was happy to have the concert next night if Miss Ogle could not stay so long in town. 'But you shall answer the note,' she told her, meaning that she should let Pacchierotti know their choice. Miss Ogle, misunderstanding, thought she was only meant to answer Mrs Castle; she had written thanking her for 'the charming note' and saying how glad she was to take advantage of her offer. Mrs Castle meanwhile assumed that she had written to Pacchierotti.

'By this unlucky want of explicitness,' wrote Susanna, 'no answer at all was sent to Pacchierotti till 2 o'clock.' On realising what had happened, Mrs Castle had immediately written a note and taken it round herself to Pacchierotti's lodgings, but by this time he had gone out. She was afraid that, having grown tired of waiting, he might have accepted some other invitation and that they would see nothing of him. As it was now nearly nine o'clock and a large party had arrived to hear him, they were all in a state of the utmost consternation. Miss Ogle, who felt the whole thing was her fault, was almost incoherent with distress. Mrs Castle, 'who muſt surely have a temper of milk and honey', joined them while Miss Ogle was the midst of her story and, though obviously upset, greeted Dr Burney with a smile. 'Oh Dr Burney, here's a roomful of people and no Pacchierotti. What is to be done?' Dr Burney did his best to comfort them, Mrs Castle begging him to keep the conversation going in the drawing room. Miss Ogle meanwhile seized on Susanna, tearfully imploring her not to leave her side, saying she would be too ashamed to show her face if Pacchierotti did not come. Susanna obligingly went with her to an upstairs room, feeling so sorry for her in her misery that she almost forgot her own disappointment.

'There seemed to be a fatality attending Mrs Caſtle's concert –' she wrote; 'among the things that chagrin'd me I reckoned the note he had written to me in the morning which I had had no opportunity to answer tho' I cd. have clear'd up his doubts of whether Mrs Castle expected him or not instantly.'

They waited upstairs, rushing out at every knock at the front door to see who it was, but to their great mortification it was never Pacchierotti. Susanna told Miss Ogle of his note to her, at which she begged Susanna to write him an answer on the spot, saying that she would get a porter to deliver it. Susanna had little hope of its being any use, since if he was at home to receive her note, he would already have had Mrs Castle's. But she did what she was asked and was just finishing her letter when a further rap at the door revived their hopes. A moment later Mrs Castle called to them up the stairs, 'Miss Ogle – Miss Burney – it's *Pacchierotti!*'

'I thought the poor Girl wd. have gone into a fit!' wrote Susanna. 'She laugh'd & cried all at once – but cd. not go down, though I long'd to be below, for several minutes – at last I persuaded her to descend – but between shame & perturbation I cd. not get her from the outward room, in wch. I met Bertoni – Mr Bath – the Dean of Winchester, & one or two more – but my Father coming in to Bertoni, & telling him Pacchierotti wd. sing now if he wd. be so good as to accompany him, Miss Ogle & I glided in & stood at the door of the Music Room during his first song.'

As Pacchierotti passed from the end of the room to the harpsichord, he saw Susanna and bowed and smiled. Miss Ogle thought it was for her. *'Sweet creature! Heaven bless him – Christ bless him!'* she kept exclaiming *sotto voce*, in a manner which made Susanna laugh whether she would or not.

Pacchierotti's opening song, *Cara Sposa* by Sacchini, was new to Susanna, 'and really so beautiful [it] gave me I think – nay I am sure of it, more pleasure than any that followed it – and tho' his voice always improves after the 1st song he began so charmingly that he left one nothing to wish'. Almost as soon as the song was over Pacchierotti made his way towards her through the crowd.

'How d'ye do, Miss Burney?'

'Oh,' cried Susanna without answering his question, 'how well you are in voice tonight Mr Pacchierotti!'

'No Ma'am,' he said smiling, 'on the contrary I have not till now sung a tune today – indeed – not since Saturday.'

'A song?' said Susanna.

'No ma'am – a tune.'

There followed a little tussle over words, Susanna explaining in French that the word 'tune' was wrong and that 'note' was the word required: 'I have not sung a note.'

'E la mia maestra,' he cried to Mrs Batt, a lady standing by.

'Ah – *une mauvaise* – a bad instructress you have,' said Susanna, and then, to account for the flustered looks of Miss Ogle, told him how worried they had been he would not come. She tried to explain the mistake over the notes, but by aiming at brevity merely puzzled him extremely. 'Very little indeed ma'am,' he said, when she asked him if he understood. Making her way into the passage outside, she then showed him the note she had been writing when he arrived. All was explained at once, and Pacchierotti told her laughing that the 'servant' who had delivered his note was in fact Bertoni. He added that he was afraid his English had been very bad. Susanna assured him that it had been perfect until near the end.

'Thursday,' she said, 'if you will give me leave we will *revise* and *correct* it.' 'If I can.' 'Oh,' she cried, no longer afraid to press him after his confidences of the previous day, 'you have promised!' He laughed and said nothing. Meanwhile Miss Ogle, who had looked ready to cry all evening and who Susanna knew was dying to speak to him, was hovering close by. Susanna explained that Miss Ogle was going to Salisbury in the next few days, and Pacchierotti talked politely of her journey, excusing himself for his bad English as he did so. 'I am sure,' said Miss Ogle, 'I never heard any English people talk so prettily.'

'Oh!' cried he, half blushing, while Miss Ogle, as if afraid of her eyes meeting his, let them wander round the room.

At this point Dr Burney and Mrs Castle came into the passage and a lively conversation ensued. Dr Burney set Pacchierotti right on some English expression, telling him that practice in the language was more important than dictionaries or grammars. 'Mais *maintenant*,' said Pacchierotti, 'comment voulez vous que je pratique?'

'We all sigh'd round I believe at the question,' wrote Susanna, 'wch. so reminded us of his departure.' The conversation continued, with Mrs Castle and her father taking the lead, Susanna joining in from time to time. Miss Ogle meanwhile did nothing but cry.

'I cannot recollect what was said,' wrote Susanna later, 'but Pacchierotti exclaimed "Oh! what clever, what sensible people there are here! – But the *best* – I beg pardon Ma'am", bowing comically to Mrs Castle, "*is* – indeed – *Dr Burney*", whom he warmly embraced while he spoke – "Go away Papa", cried I laughing – "can you stand that?" – and accordingly they both ran away laughing together into the other room, but they had not the cruelty to stay away long, & P renewed his Compts. to the English people at his return & added. "*I lament myself to go because I cannot admire them enough.*"'

Miss Rumbold, a friend of the Burneys, and 'a fat frightful woman' who was with her now joined the party, and the little passage became so full that they all adjourned to the next room. Miss Ogle, who had begged Susanna not to leave her – 'which indeed I never did, but for a few moments to speak to Mrs & Miss Ord' – got a quiet seat for herself by the harpsichord, where Charles Rousseau Burney began to play. Pacchierotti meanwhile, 'was surrounded by fair females, & particularly Miss Rumbold & her fat companion who stuck to him like a burr'; he eventually disengaged himself by coming behind the harpsichord to join Dr Burney and two or three others. He was then implored to sing again, and though the aria requested, *Te Seguiro*, was not one he would normally have chosen, he good-naturedly agreed. After this refreshments were handed round. Susanna accompanied Mrs Castle and Miss Ogle into a cooler room, where Pacchierotti joined them. They were followed by Miss Rumbold and his 'fat conquest', which so enraged Miss Ogle that she called out to Susanna: '*Confound her!* – See how she pesters him – an ugly nasty fat creature – I am sure he can't like her!' 'I don't believe he did,' wrote Susanna, 'but it was impossible hear such expressions and not to laugh.'

Susanna tried to change the conversation, asking Pacchierotti when his final appearance at the opera house would be, as she was determined not to miss it. It was then that he told her of Sheridan's plan that he should extend their contract by giving another performance on July 1st: 'I cannot refuse him such a request but I wish he would deal with me accordingly.'

He then turned to Miss Ogle, who was now weeping openly, and with 'infinite delicacy' tried to console her for having to leave town: 'You have so many friends to part with – because you need *but* to be *known* and seen to have friends – you need not like Diogenes, and like as I ought to, *to take a lanthorn to search for your friends in the midst of the day* – But it is for your friends to mourn your loss, not you! – If you weep for your departure, who will return here next winter – Oh how must I bear it when the time comes, my own?'

'I shan't come to town next year,' said Miss Ogle, 'I am sure I shan't care about it – for if I was here I would never go to the opera.'

'Oh Ma'am,' said Pacchierotti, half surprised and half affected by her wildness, 'You muſt not punish yourself…'

'Oh – it would only be a punishment to me to go.'

'Indeed – if you believe me – your condition then would be better than now.'

'Oh don't say that Signor Pacchierotti,' said she, 'you cannot think it.'

'In my humble opinion…' began Pacchierotti.

'Here he ſtopt,' wrote Susanna, 'he cd. not carry on such a falsehood any longer.'

They all moved to the harpsichord, where Pacchierotti sang a minuet of Bertoni's – 'the moſt common thing that can be imagined,' wrote Susanna, 'but he sang divinely and everyone seemed to liſten with rapture.' Poor Miss Ogle, both during and after the song, was saying 'such things that not to laugh was impossible', though Susanna did all she could to persuade her to be quiet since everyone was listening.

Miss Ogle was quite unabashed. All the servants in her own house and Mrs Castle's, she said, were laughing at the anxiety she had been in all day. 'Great fools! because they thought it was *all owing to my being so much in love with him* – but to be sure it can't be *that* – you know – but I don't know – there is such an innocence about him, and in his situation – that…Indeed I *do* love him – I should like to live with him all my life – & be his friend.'

'Did you ever hear the like?' asked Susanna. Fortunately Bertoni was standing by, and she was able to pass off Miss Ogle's hysterics with a joke. *'Voila une autre Signora Susanna,'* she said, *'qui se meurt parcequ'elle s'en va à la campagne et qu'elle ne pourra plus entendre de la musique.'* 'Ah,' cried Bertoni to Pacchierotti, *'Ecco una buona signora Susanna.'* Susanna laughed and Miss Ogle, half unwillingly joined in. *'Le due Susanna ridono,'* he said to Dr Burney, and Susanna was obliged to make up some nonsense to explain their laughter.

There had been a longish pause after Pacchierotti's last song, and every one was standing round expectantly. 'For God's sake play something, Dr Burney,' cried Miss Ogle, 'We shall have all the people go!'

Dr Burney good naturedly took his seat at the harpsichord. Pacchierotti nonetheless took up his hat and approached them to take leave of them – chiefly of Miss Ogle, whose peculiar behaviour had visibly struck and interested him.

'He showed not the *slightest* appearance of vanity,' wrote Susanna, 'tho' she had done everything possible to raise that passion in him, but looked at her with a respectful mixture of concern and tenderness.'

'Beg him not to go,' said Miss Ogle to Susanna in a low voice, with her eyes full of tears.

'Il ne fait pas si tard, Signor Pacchierotti,' said Susanna.

Pacchierotti told her that he was obliged to be out extremely early next morning and that it was now was past eleven. Then turning to Miss Ogle he said to her, 'May all the blessings of heaven be poured down upon you.'

'Don't go – don't go yet!' she cried, almost without knowing what she was saying.

'I am more sorry than I can express to go,' said Pacchierotti, and considering her and the state she was in with a look of surprise and concern, he stood for a moment or two quite still, 'then turned,' wrote Susanna, '& sd. something but I heard not what to Bertoni who exclaimed *"veramente poverina!"* – bowing then to me they went to speak to Mrs Castle & slid out of the room.'

It is the last we see of Pacchierotti, and with the bustling away of the hysterical Miss Ogle, Susanna's journal comes to an end. A few days later she was joined by Fanny, somewhat to the pique of Mrs Thrale. 'Fanny Burney goes home now to study & live recluse,' she wrote sarcastically in *Thraliana*, '& I tell her to kiss Pacchierotti – the Castrato singer of whom that family is so fond.' Perhaps Mrs Thrale was already influenced by the jealous Piozzi, who had become 'a prodigious Favourite' of hers and whom, to the great scandal and confusion of her family and friends, she would marry after the death of her husband three years later.

Pacchierotti left London on July 8. We have no further record of his last days in London, of his final performances or of his farewells to Susanna. Did Fanny destroy the remaining pages of her sister's journal when she came to edit her family's papers? She always took care to censor anything that might bring discredit or embarrassment to the Burneys. It has long been suggested that Susanna was in love with Pacchierotti; certainly her feeling for him and her passionate admiration for his artistry provide the emotional undercurrent which carries her narrative along. It would of course have been an unfulfilled and hopeless love, but none the less real for that; it may well be that Dr Burney, sensing the growing intimacy between them, was secretly relieved that Pacchierotti would not be coming back to London the following year. But before long Lieutenant Phillips, virile, impetuous, with all the panache of a returning hero, would appear to sweep Susanna off her feet. With the arrival of Cook's last expedition in October 1780, another chapter in her life would begin.

XIII

Susanna spent August with her father and Charlotte and Fanny as guests of Mr Crisp at Chesington Hall. Fanny, with all hopes of seeing *The Witlings* produced behind her, was about to embark on a new novel, *Cecilia*, urged on by Crisp and Dr Burney. She intended to spend most of the autumn at Chesington, working on her book away from interruptions and distractions. Mrs Thrale accepted her absence grudgingly but kept up an animated correspondence with her. 'Dr Burney says your letters and mine are alike,' she told her, 'and that it comes by writing so incessantly to each other.'

On September 24, Mr Crisp, in a letter to his sister, reported that Dr Burney had received a letter from Jem in the Orkneys, his first in four years. The return of the expedition would bring a crop of promotions: Jem was confirmed in his rank as a commander; Gore and King became post captains,

King taking up Cook's vacant position on the naval establish-
ment of Greenwich Hospital; Molesworth Phillips became
a captain of marines. Even though the tragic outcome of the
voyage was already known and the essential purpose of the
expedition, the discovery of a northern passage through the
Arctic, had not been achieved, the *Resolution* and the *Discovery*
received a hero's welcome when they arrived. No sooner had
they docked at Deptford than they were besieged by a crowd
of sightseers and friends. Mr Thrale was one of those who travelled down to see the famous ships, bringing an invitation to
Jem to join them at Streatham when Fanny was next staying
there. Dr Johnson too announced his intention of visiting him
on board. It is not certain whether Johnson did so, but he must
have met Jem shortly after, for Mrs Thrale, in a letter to Fanny,
records him as pronouncing an 'eulogium' of her brother: 'how
amiable he was, and how gentle in his manner, &c., tho' he had
lived so many years with sailors and savages'.

Dr Burney was quietly proud of his eldest son. 'Appre-
hensions for his safety had long kept me comfortless & for
some time hopeless,' he wrote to his old friend Thomas Twin-
ing, '– however he is now safe in old England and arrived in
the Thames, master and Commander of the ship the *Discovery*,
of which he went out Lieut. He is an honest worthy young
man, & if I may be allowed the expression, as good a Seaman
& Subject as I could wish him to be. I really believe him to
know his business thoroughly.'

It was enthralling to pore over Jem's charts and journals
and to hear of his experiences on the journey home: a volcanic
eruption, amid thunder and lightning, on the Kamchatkan
coast; the funeral of Captain Clerke at Petropavlosk, attended
by all the Russian garrison; bear hunting with the Kamchadale
Indians; shooting walrus on the arctic ice-floes; bartering
otter skins for tea and porcelain in Canton. He had brought

121

back presents – fabrics and feathers from the South Seas, a Kamchatka puppy (much coveted by Mrs Thrale), a monkey from Sumatra for his small brother Dick. 'What language can it speak,' asked Mrs Thrale facetiously, '*chattering* perhaps.'

London was in the throes of South Sea fever. John Webber gave a preliminary display of his sketches on the voyage; he would later work them up into finished drawings to accompany the Admiralty's official account of the expedition. Fanny spent a satisfying morning looking at his views of Tahiti, Kamchatka, New Zealand and China, together with portraits of their various inhabitants and a collection of curiosities brought back from his travels. Captain King did the honours, Fanny finding him one of the 'most natural, gay, honest and pleasant characters' she had ever met. Mrs Thrale planned a splendid court dress, inspired by a native Hawaiian garment Jem had brought back from his previous South Sea voyage, and took to calling Fanny her 'dearest Tyo' – the name, according to Jem, used by the Tahitians when they adopted an English sailor as a chosen friend or brother.

St Martin's Street, as always, was an open house for visitors, and Jem's friends inevitably made their way there. It was perhaps surprising that Williamson was one of them, but Jem was easy-going and Williamson far from sensitive. Susanna had ceased writing her journal (or perhaps her entries were destroyed) but a page inserted at the back of the volume describes Williamson's visit. She found him good looking and showily dressed but in all other respects detestable. 'He swore furiously…told stories of himself without end – some of a swaggering, puffing sort – others really disgraceful to himself tho' he meant them otherwise, & spoke of English women in raptures, comparing them to those of the South Seas in terms so indelicate & gross that I was thoroughly disgusted with him.'

He added to his offences by abusing every one he mentioned. 'I know he spoke highly of James,' she wrote, 'and otherwise took it for granted he wd. say no harm of him – but I own I expected every minute some disagreable compliment to poor Phillips wch. tho' from that quarter it wd. have merited no regard, wd. yet have discomposed me a little before all those people.'

Susanna had met Phillips with her brother almost immediately after his return. There seems to have been a instant attraction between them, Susanna perhaps on the rebound from her emotional involvement with Pacchierotti, Phillips, from his close friendship with Jem, with a strong prepossession for his sister. We only know of their courtship elliptically, in letters from Fanny and Mrs Thrale. There are none from Susanna to tell the tale, but in the course of the autumn of 1780 she became secretly engaged to Phillips. It was important that the story should not reach the gossip columns – as pernicious then as now. Phillips' appointment as captain had yet to be confirmed, his financial position was far from clear. There was talk of an entailed property in Ireland which was expected to revert to him, but his uncle, the current occupant, was still very much alive, and his only certain income was his service pay. Dr Burney was doubtful, Susanna herself was in a 'horrid twitter' lest Mrs Thrale, Fanny's confidante, should give her away. 'She charges me,' wrote Fanny, 'to remind you that her secret is a real secret at present, & that she should be strongly uneasy to have it spread abroad, as connections of that sort hanging long in suspense occasion a thousand disagreable conjectures and impertinent wonderments.'

It was this that had made Susanna embarrassed when listening to Williamson abuse his shipmates. Unexpectedly however he had nothing bad to say about Phillips, beyond imitating him, 'drolly enough, and I doubt not like enough', poring over his music in their shipboard concerts. 'He won his fiddle once of him, he sd., for a bet, but let him have it again. "I could have kept it", sd. he, "if that wd. have put an end to his music – but d—n it, he'd have made a fiddle of his own in a fortnight and that would have been worse than ever!"'

In Susanna's later journals when she was married and living in Surrey, she often mentioned Phillips's 'shop', in which he spent many hours with a lathe, turning and making things in wood. According to Crisp, who met him shortly after their engagement, he was 'a moſt ingenious Creature; and such a Gentleman mechanic I believe is not in the Kingdom; he has presented the Museum with Models of a vaſt Variety of Vessels, Utensils, Arms &c., &c., &c., executed with his own hand alone with a degree of neatness and accuracy that cannot be surpassed…These models are of the many uncommon things he met with in going round the world.' The museum is not specified, but may well have been the British Museum; from the reminiscences of Mrs Lefroy, daughter of one of Phillips' shipmates, we learn that he was a frequent visitor there and 'was ever to be seen lounging and offering advice, or a hand whenever any novelty arrived'.

Crisp had taken a good view of Phillips, finding him 'a noble, brave, open, agreable Fellow but 26', adding perhaps rather optimistically that he seemed to have a natural turn for economy 'when not led away by high Spirits or Company'. It was a faint intimation of trouble ahead though Fanny, at the time, was equally satisfied with her sister's choice. 'Indeed my beloved Susy,' she wrote from Chesington, 'nothing gives me more true happiness, nothing in the world *can* give me more, than your fair and moſt desirable prospeĉts with this *sweet-blooded* young man, God bless you both!' But though she was happy for Susanna, she dreaded the impending separation from her sister:

'There is something to me at the thought of being so near parting with you as the inmate of the same house – room – Bed – confidence & life, that is not very merrifying, though I would by no means have things altered. Oh far from it!'

To make matters worse Fanny was tied down by her novel, writing under pressure from her father and Mr Crisp, who was determined to keep her at Chesington Hall till it was finished. It was good to be away from her stepmother's 'bright art of tormenting', but she longed to be with her sister to help her smooth away the difficulties surrounding her marriage. 'The Capitano has lately been promoted, & is now very anxious to accelerate matters,' she told Mrs Thrale, 'but my Father, very anxious & fearful for poor Susanna, does not think there is *de quoi manger* very plentifully. For my own part, I think they could do very well, I know Susan is a very good economiſt, & I know there is not any part of my Family that cannot live upon very little as chearfully as moſt folks upon very much.' Susanna, she added, did nothing to push things forward – 'so she does depend upon *friends' professions*; and if she had none in the world, never I am sure, would she look to herself'.

Meanwhile Jem had joined Fanny at Chesington Hall, 'glad of a little reſt and quiet and country Air…after being a Tennis Ball round the Globe for four years and a half' and delighting Mr Crisp by his tales of the South Seas. Other guests arrived from time to time, including the Miss Paynes, daughters of Fanny's future publisher Thomas Payne, whose little L shaped bookshop in Castle Street, near St-Martin-in-the-Fields, was a favourite resort for London's men of letters. Before long Jem was courting the youngest of the two sisters, Sally. 'Jem has made some progress in his attempt at laying close seige to Sally Payne,' wrote Crisp to his sister when Jem returned to London, 'for in a letter from Suzette she says: "James has dined in Caſtle Street *only four times* since he came to town (N.B. he has been in town five days.)'"The two became engaged soon after, though the marriage did not take place for several years.

Both Jem's and Phillips's courtships were interrupted by the call of duty. The war with the American colonies, as well as with France, Spain and Holland, was still continuing, though no one believed it could go on much longer. On November 2, 1781, while Jem, on a visit to Chesington, was sitting down to play cards after tea, an express arrived from London with an order from the Admiralty appointing him as temporary captain of the *Latona*, 'one of the beſt frigates in the Navy, of thirty eight guns, and immediately...ready for service'.

'Jem was almoſt frantic with ecſtasy of joy,' wrote Fanny to Mrs Thrale; 'he sang, laughed, drank to his own success and danced about the room with Miss Kitty till he put her quite out of breath. His hope is to go out immediately, and have a brush with some of the Dons, Monsieurs, or Mynheers while he is in possession of a ship of sufficient force to attack any frigate he may meet.'

A few weeks later it was Phillips's turn to be called up. 'I really don't see much hope that he *can* escape the summons,' wrote Fanny to the worried Susanna, 'as I see by the Papers a general order to all officers to repair to quarters. However he will go *nowhere* for long, that I think we may be sure, as a Peace muſt be speedy though, & indeed for that very reason all war-like preparations muſt be carried on with more vigour than ever, that our terms may be less humiliating.'

Fanny was expressing the general opinion. In October, 1781, almost all that remained of the British army in America had surrendered to Washington at Yorktown. From then on, though American independence was not recognised for a further year, the war was only maintained on principle, without hope of success. Jem saw no sign of the enemy during his temporary command of the *Latona*. Sent to patrol the waters between the coasts of Scotland and Norway, he encountered such violent storms that for several weeks he was forced to take shelter off the southernmost point of Norway and in March 1782, after 'a terrible cruise, much danger, infinite sickness and no prize', was relieved of his vicarious captainship by Captain the Honourable H.S.Conway – a galling reminder that the Burneys, though distinguished in the arts, lacked the right aristocratic connections when it came to naval matters.

By this time Susanna's marriage had taken place. The Captain was released on leave: the intervention of his married sister, Mrs Shirley, who agreed to loan her brother £400 against his expectations from his uncle, had dealt with Dr Burney's chief objections, and he had reluctantly given his consent.

'Next Thursday [the day of Burney's weekly music lesson with Queeney] will you dearest Madam, dispense with seeing my Father?' wrote Fanny to Mrs Thrale from St Martin's Street, in early January, 1782, 'or must Captain Phillips dispense with receiving his wife? – that is the alternative…Here, we are all bustle & hurry. The Shirleys and a prodigious tribe of Burneys &c. dine here on Thursday – mighty disagreable arrangement for Susan but hardly to be avoided.'

On January 10, 1782, Susanna and Captain Phillips were married at St Martin-in-the-Fields. Dr Burney gave her away, the Reverend Charles Shirley, Phillips's brother-in-law officiated. Despite Dr Burney's doubts, the Captain, or 'Cappy', as they called him, was soon a general favourite with the family, even the sour Mrs Burney unbending in his jovial company. For her step-children she remained as difficult as ever. 'Nothing is said that she does not fly into a Passion at and Contradict…' complained the forthright Charlotte, '*Whatever is is Wrong!* That's her Maxim.'

The young couple spent their first days together with

Mr Crisp at Chesington, then Susanna began the life of a marine captain's wife, packing up her possessions and following Phillips from one recruiting centre to another. Mrs Thrale, recently widowed and struggling with the difficulties of dealing with her husband's estate, was eager to lure Fanny back to Streatham in the hopes of taking 'Susannucia's place' in her heart. But Fanny was still completing her novel and dreaded the distractions of dress and visits which staying there would entail. In any case, there was no one who could take her sister's place.

'O my dear Susy, if I was but to tell you how I miss you at Home!' she wrote a few months after Susanna's marriage. 'I did not know how *singularly* our two minds were blended, till you were thus removed: but I want to say something to you every Hour – Nobody else ever cared so much to hear me, nor do I find anybody else to whom I care so much to speak. Dear Hetty [Esther], whom so tenderly I love, is so absorbed in family matters of her own – our good Charlotte, who has the trueſt affeƈtion for me, which warmly I return, *means* to supply your place, but has not the powers – our taſtes do not naturally accord, our likings, our dislikings are often disimilar – we don't admire the same people, we don't read the same Books, we don't search the same amusements, we don't adore the same Pacchierotti.'

The great singer had come back to the King's Theatre (where Sheridan's chaotic reign had ended the previous year) for the season of 1781-82 and was once again a frequent visitor at St Martin's Street; he remained a beloved friend of the family, but Fanny's letters only give us fleeting glimpses of him. He was eager to read her new novel, the first volume of which was already completed. 'My father himself told Pac of his reading and fondness for the firſt volume,' she wrote to Susanna shortly after her marriage, '– & Pac is half wild with joy & eagerness! he desires, he says, "to pry a *littel* into so great work!" He charged me to give you his best & affectionate compliments.'

Cecilia was finally published by Jem's future father-in-law Thomas Payne in June 1782. With its scenes of bankruptcy, suicide and madness, it was a darker book than the enchanting *Evelina*, though its gallery of characters was as lively as before. Its success confirmed Fanny Burney's fame as a writer; at a party in Brighton soon after, she wrote, she found herself as much an object of curiosity as Omai. Susanna and Captain Phillips read the novel over with her when she stayed with them that summer. It was the happiest possible visit, Susanna pregnant and glowingly content, the Captain full of brotherly attentions. The three of them talked 'treason' of La Dama, Phillips full of indignation at what Susanna had had to suffer and satisfaction at having rescued her from tyranny.

For Pacchierotti, whose arrival in London opened a new round of triumphs – 'everybody says [he] is much finer than when he was here two years ago,' wrote one admirer, Lady Mary Coke – *Cecilia* brought a moment of literary immortality. He is included in the novel, in his own person, when as part of the heroine's initiation into polite society, she attends a rehearsal at the opera house and hears him sing for the first time:

'The surprise and pleasure which she [Cecilia] received from the performance in general, were faint, cold and languid compared to the strength of those emotions excited by Signore Pacchierotti in particular; and though not one half of the excellencies of that superior singer were necessary either to amaze or charm her unaccustomed ears, though the refinement of his taste and masterly originality of his genius, to be praised as they deserved, called for the judgement and knowledge of professors, yet a natural love for music in some measure supplied the place of cultivation, and what she could neither explain or understand, she could feel and enjoy.

'The opera was *Artaserse*, and the pleasure she received from the music was much augmented by her previous acquaintance with that interesting drama; yet, as to all noviciates in science, whatever is least complicated is most pleasing, she found herself by nothing so deeply impressed, as by the plaintive and beautiful simplicity with which Pacchierotti uttered the affecting repetition of *sono innocente!* his voice, always either sweet or impassioned, delivered those words in a tone of softness, pathos and sensibility, that struck her with a sensation not more new than delightful.'

Susanna's marriage, which began so happily, and which brought her three beloved children, would end in disaster. Captain Phillips' affairs did not prosper, he was put on half pay, he borrowed heavily from his father-in-law, he became increasingly surly and bad tempered. Perhaps there was some inherent instability in his character, perhaps the violent experiences he had undergone on Cook's last voyage had left their mark.

For a few years they settled in Surrey, in the little village of Mickleham, living close to Fanny's friends the Lockes, whose house at Norbury Park was a centre of culture and civilised conversation. It was staying here, as has been said, that Fanny first met the little group of liberal French aristocrats, including the former Minister of War, Narbonne, who had been forced to flee from the terrors of the Revolution and had found a temporary refuge with Madame de Staël at Juniper Hall nearby. Susanna, whose charm and sympathy helped console the shattered exiles, was the darling of the group – 'the sweetest, the most intelligent' of companions in the words of Narbonne. (Madame de Staël, who had abandoned her husband to follow Narbonne to England, accused him of being in love with her.) It was Narbonne's friend and chief of staff, the

Chevalier d'Arblay, who would become Fanny's husband the following year. 'And NEVER – NEVER,' wrote Fanny, 'was union more exquisitely blessed and felicitious – though after the first 8 years of unmingled happiness, it was assailed by many calamities – chiefly of separation or illness – but never mentally unbroken.'

For Susanna there was no such happy ending. In 1795, Phillips was obliged to go to Ireland, where he had finally inherited a property in County Louth and where the unsettled conditions – threats of invasion from the French and rebellion among his fellow countrymen – made his presence essential. Susanna was forced to follow him on pain of separation from her children; he had already taken her elder son Norbury with him and placed him with a private tutor in Dublin. Susanna's health had always been fragile; in the damp and discomfort of the dilapidated, half furnished house she found there she became ill, probably with consumption, the disease from which her mother had died.

Fanny destroyed most of Susanna's letters from Ireland, just as she had destroyed the earlier letters relating to what she termed the 'fatal' marriage. Only fourteen remained selected, she wrote on the folder containing them, 'from a beautiful series which, from various motives, F d'A has deemed it a duty to destroy. These preserved were written from Jan. 17 1797 – Decr. 1799.' By this time Susanna was forced to hide her correspondence from her husband, who was not only flagrantly pursuing another woman but deeply suspicious of her family and friends like the Lockes who, growing increasingly desperate at the failing state of her health, were begging her to return to England. Her letters describe the frequent storms in their relationship (she referred to Phillips as *'Le Temps'*), his irrational tyranny, his mounting debts, her fears and uncertainties as the rebellion of 1798 swept Ireland. County Louth was fortunately spared from violence, though Phillips had prepared for the worst by joining the local militia; but its flat dull landscape, broken by two or three steeples, with a distant view of the sea – the sea which divided Susanna from her family in England – made a mournful background to her feelings of loneliness and separation. At night, she tried to soothe herself to sleep by following her sister's advice to go over pieces of music and poetry in her head – 'but *en fait de vers,*' she told Fanny, 'one poem constantly forces itself on my recollection – the Hymn to Adversity…and the train of thoughts which follow are not friendly to rest.' In the end, her health and spirits deteriorated so much that even Phillips realised the seriousness of her situation and agreed to accompany her and two of the children (Norbury remaining in Dublin with his tutor) back to her father's house in England.

Her last letter from Ireland, written in a wavering hand that showed her increasing weakness, spoke of her eagerness to see her sister and her family again: 'do not worry at my ill writing – I have a bad pen,' she told them in a vain attempt at reassurance. But it was already late December, and the journey in bad weather across the Irish Sea was probably the final straw. When they arrived at Parkgate near Chester, the most convenient port available, Susanna was dying. Her brother Charles arrived just in time to support her in her last few days, but the roads were so blocked by snow and ice that Fanny could not reach her. Susanna died without seeing her sister, on January 6, 1800.

Epilogue

Fanny would always keep the day of Susanna's death, the day that marked the end of her 'perfect Happiness on earth', as one of solitude and mourning. None of the rest of the family could bring themselves to speak to Phillips, the dashing 'Capitano' who had seemed such an ideal husband at first and who, it must be said, had made Susanna very happy during the first ten years of their marriage. Only Jem remained loyal to his old friend, in later years a frequent guest at his house in James Street, where he is remembered by Charles Lamb, another frequent visitor, as a battered but lusty veteran, 'still sending out cartels of defiance at old Time'. For Fanny, the very idea that Jem could receive him was revolting. 'Not one moment's penitence has ever appeared to soften off his crime or plead for his forgiveness.' Certainly his actions after Susanna's death did him no credit. He married again within a year, only to desert his second wife and children for a mistress. Nor does it seem that he ever repaid Dr Burney the money Burney had lent him, a serious matter for the doctor, who had seven other children to provide for. Often in debt, Phillips was occasionally saved from the bailiffs by former shipmates such as Jem.

Jem died in 1821, having reached the rank of Rear-Admiral on the retired list – he had been retired on grounds of ill health in 1785 – and having written a five volume account of his voyages, *A Chronological History of Discoveries in the South Seas or Pacific Ocean*, which remains the standard work on the subject. His obituaries paid tribute to his achievements as an explorer and to the humanity which, in an age of harsh naval disci-

133

pline, he had always shown towards his men. In his will he left instructions that Phillips should be one of only four mourners to follow his coffin to the grave. Phillips organised Jem's funeral – which his sisters did not attend – and arranged for a bust to be made from his death mask, which he kept with him for the rest of his life. He died in 1832, the last survivor of Cook's third voyage, expressing a wish on his deathbed to be buried in the same grave as Jem, his 'earliest and most respected friend'.

Pacchierotti continued to be a devoted friend of the Burneys, exchanging letters with them over the years and seeing them regularly when he sang in London. During his last engagement there he coincided with Haydn, on the first of his visits to England, and Lord Mount Edgcumbe in his musical reminiscences recalls a memorable evening when Pacchierotti was persuaded by Haydn to perform his solo cantata *Ariadne auf Naxos*, the composer playing the pianoforte part. 'It is needless to say,' wrote Mount Edgecumbe, 'that the performance was perfect.'

Pachierotti's last public appearance was at the opening of the Fenice theatre in Venice in 1792. But he came out of retirement twice, once to sing before Napoleon in 1806 and once in 1814, at the age of seventy four, to sing at the requiem for Bertoni in St Mark's. It was a moving occasion, for not only had Bertoni been his teacher and lifelong friend, but Pacchierotti had made his début at the cathedral nearly fifty years before.

Pacchierotti was almost the last of the great castrati. There was a growing revulsion of humanitarian opinion against the practice of castration for purely musical purposes. Meanwhile critics in Europe were beginning to complain about the artificiality of the castrato voice; by the last years of the eighteenth century male sopranos were beginning to be replaced by tenors. As romantic opera took the place of *opera seria,* castrato singers were less in demand, though Pacchierotti, whose voice spanned three octaves and who was equally at home in the tenor as the soprano range, remained sought after to the end. At the same time the custom by which singers created their own virtuoso embellishments to the printed score went out of favour. The art of spontaneous improvisation which had been one of the glories of the castrato's singing, was no longer part of the singer's repertoire. Composers now preferred to set down every note themselves; if in the eighteenth century the composer could be called the servant of the singer, by the early nineteenth century the singer had become the servant of the composer.

Pacchierotti spent an honoured old age, retiring to Padua where Rossini came to pay him homage, and Stendhal found him still sublime at seventy. 'I have learnt more about music in six conversations with this great artist,' wrote Stendhal, 'than through any book; it is soul speaking to soul.'

A hundred years later another distinguished visitor, Violet Paget, writing under the pseudonym of Vernon Lee, redis-covered Pacchierotti's villa, the former palazzo of Cardinal Bembo, half lost in 'a beautiful tangle of trees and grass and flowers'.

'Of all those dim figures of long forgotten singers,' she wrote, 'which arise, tremulous and hazy, from out of the faded pages of biographies and scores, evoked by some intense word of admiration, or some pathetic snatch of melody, there is one more poetical than the rest – for all such ghosts of forgotten genius are poetical – that of Gasparo Pacchierotti.'

The gardener showed her round his house, 'a battered house, covered with creepers and amphorae, and sentimental inscriptions from the works of the poets and philosophers of a hundred years ago.' He showed her into a long narrow room in which was a large slender harpsichord – the harpsichord, he told her, which had belonged to Pacchierotti. He then led her into a darkened lumber room where hung the portrait of the singer, thickly covered with dust: 'a mass of dark blurs, from out of which appeared scarcely more than the pale thin face – a face with deep dreamy eyes and tremulously tender lips, full of vague, wistful, contemplative poetry, as if of aspirations after something sweeter, fairer – aspirations never fulfilled but never disappointed, and forming in themselves a kind of perfection.'

The memory of Pacchierotti is still more distant now. We can never recapture the transcendent beauty of the castrato voice, or the strangeness and glamour which surrounded these vanished, almost unimaginable creatures. But Susanna Burney's journal, with its detailed, heartfelt picture of one of the greatest of them all, brings us perhaps as close as we can get.

Books Consulted[†]

Alexander, Michael, *Omai, 'Noble Savage'*, 1977

Arblay, Madame d' (Fanny Burney), *Evelina*, Penguin Classics edition, 1994
    Cecilia, World's Classics edition, 1988
    Memoirs of Dr Burney, 1832
    The Diary and Letters of Madame d'Arblay, edited by Charlotte Barrett, 1905, 6 vols.

Balderston, K.C., ed, *Thraliana: the Diary of Mrs Hester Lynch Thrale (later Mrs Piozzi)*, 1942

Barbier, Patrick, *The World of the Castrati*, trs. Margaret Crosland, 1996

Barry, John, ed., *The Voyages of Captain Cook*, Wordsworth Classics edition, 1999

Beaglehole, J.C., *The Life of Captain James Cook*, 1974

Burney, Dr Charles, *A General History of Music*, 4 vols., 1776-89
    Letters of Dr Charles Burney, 1751-1784, Oxford, 1991

Clifford, James, *Hester Lynch Piozzi (Mrs Thrale)*, Oxford, 1941

Chisholm, Kate, *Fanny Burney: Her Life*, 1994

Christiansen, Rupert, *Prima Donna*, 1984

Derwent, Lord, *Rossini and some forgotten nightingales*, 1934

Doody, Margaret Anne, *Fanny Burney, 1752-1840, A Biography*, New Brunswick, 1968

Farr, Evelyn, *The World of Fanny Burney*, 1993

The New Grove Dictionary of Music and Musicians, ed. Stanley Sadie, 1980

Harman, Claire, *Fanny Burney*, 2000

Hemlow, Joyce, *The History of Fanny Burney*, Oxford, 1958

Hemlow, Joyce, with Jeanne M. Burgess & Althea Douglas, *A Catalogue of the Burney Family Correspondence, 1749-1878*, New Brunswick, 1971

Hill, Constance, *The House in St Martin's Street*, 1907

Hough, Richard, *Captain James Cook*, 1994

Hutton, W.H., ed, *Burford Papers: Being Letters of Samuel Crisp to his sister at Burford and Other Studies of a Century (1745-1845)*, 1905

Hyde, Mary, *The Thrales of Streatham Park*, Cambridge, Mass, 1977

Johnson, R.B. *Fanny Burney and the Burneys*, 1926

Kelly, Linda, *Juniper Hall: An English Refuge from the French Revolution*, 1991
    Richard Brinsley Sheridan, 1997

Kilpatrick, Sarah, *Fanny Burney*, Newton Abbot, 1980

Lamb, Charles, *The Essays of Elia*, ed. Alfred Ainger, 1910

Lee, Vernon (Violet Paget), *Studies of the Eighteenth Century in Italy*, 1907

---

†All books published in London, unless stated otherwise.

Macaulay, Lord, *Essays* (Essay on Mme d'Arblay), 1886

Manwaring, G.C., *My Friend the Admiral, the Life and Letters of Rear-Admiral James Burney*, 1931

Mount Edgecumbe, Earl of, *Musical Reminiscences, containing an account of the Italian Opera in England, from 1773*, 1834

Mowl, Timothy, *William Beckford*, 1998

The Oxford Companion to Music, ed. Percy A. Scholes, revised by John Owen Ward, Oxford, 1970, 20 vols.

The Oxford Dictionary of Opera, ed. John Warrack and Ewan West, Oxford, 1992

Pleasants, Henry, *The Great Singers: from the dawn of opera to our own time*, 1967

Porter, Roy, ed., *England in the Eighteenth Century*, 1998

Price, Curtis, Judith Milhous and Robert D. Hume, *Italian Opera in Late Eighteenth Century London. Vol i: The King's Theatre, Haymarket, 1778-1791*, Oxford, 1993

Rohr, Deborah, *The Careers of British Musicians, 1850-1850*, Cambridge, 2001

Scholes, Percy A., *The Great Dr Burney: His Life, His Travels, his Works and his Friends*, Oxford, 1948

Sheridan, Richard Brinsley, *Plays*, ed. Cecil Price, Oxford, 1989

Sitwell, Sacheverell, *Southern Baroque Art: A Study of Painting, Architecture and Music in Italy and Spain in the 17th and 18th Centuries*, 1924

Stendhal, *The Life of Rossini*, trs. Richard N. Coe, 1985

Watson, J. Steven, *The Reign of George III, 1992*

CATALOGUES & PERIODICALS

Great Explorers: Captain Cook and his Exploration of the Pacific,
National Maritime Museum and H.M. Bark Endeavour Foundation, 1998

James Barry: The Artist as Hero, William L. Pressly, Tate Gallery, 1983

Annual Register, 1832 (Obituary of Captain Phillips)

Gentleman's Magazine, 1832, ii (Obituary of Captain Phillips)

MANUSCRIPTS

British Library: The Barrett Collection of Burney Papers, Egerton MS: Letter Journal of Susan Phillips (Burney), 3691; Letters from Frances d'Arblay (Burney) to Mrs Thrale, 3695, f.61 iv; Letters from Susan Phillips to Frances d'Arblay, 3695, f.63 v.

The Berg Collection of English and American Literature, the New York Public Library, Astor, Lenox and Tilden Foundations: Letters from Frances d'Arblay to her sister Susanna Elizabeth Phillips, August 1780-April 1782; Letters from Susanna Elizabeth Phillips, January 1797-December 1799.

WEBSITE

Burney Olleson: includes extracts from Susanna Burney's letter-journals and details of a long term project for web publication of her complete journals and letters under the editorship of Dr Philip Olleson, University of Nottingham.
http://www.nottingham.ac.uk/hrc/projects/burney/

ILLUSTRATIONS

Cover: courtesy of the National Portrait Gallery and of the British Library.

Page 5: 'The Death of Captain Cook' by John Webber: courtesy of the Royal Geographic Society. (Molesworth Phillips is in the foreground.)

Page 40: 'The Sunday Concert' by Charles Lorraine Smith: courtesy of the British Museum. (Pacchierotti with sheet-music is behind the keyboard; Dr Burney is conversing with a lady, bottom right.)

Page 81: The burning of Newgate Prison during the Gordon Riots: from a contemporary print.

Page 120: 'Susanna Phillips' by her cousin Edward Francesco Burney, circa 1789; courtesy of the National Portrait Gallery.

Page 136: Gasparo Pacchierotti, drawn in London in 1782: courtesy of the Royal College of Music.